LEADERSHIP FOR LEADERS

LEADERSHIP FOR LEADERS

A SMART APPROACH TO INSPIRE REAL EXCELLENCE

Arthur Gill

For the steadfast visionaries who guide others toward success, one ambitious goal at a time...

Table of Contents

FOREWORD

Welcome, esteemed leader, to a book crafted precisely for someone of your unique caliber. Whether you've just stepped into a leadership role or are looking to hone your well-seasoned skills, *Leadership for Leaders: A Smart Approach to Inspire Real Excellence* is designed to guide you through the finer points of managing with vision, authority, and (let's not mince words) just the right amount of pressure. After all, leadership isn't just about the destination; it's about inspiring your team every step of the way, making sure they know you're in control, and ensuring they recognize exactly who is setting the standard.

In these pages, you'll explore the art of setting expectations so high they inspire awe (and occasional panic!), redefining accountability as a team sport, and fostering resilience through the subtle encouragement of controlled chaos. Each strategy is a testament to the creative approaches modern leaders must sometimes embrace.

Great leaders are always open to learning, and if there's one thing this book guarantees, it's a fresh perspective on how to push boundaries, test limits, and drive results—whether or not your team realizes how essential those limits and boundaries are. Embrace the challenges presented here, and take these principles to heart; they are designed to make a lasting impact on you and, naturally, on those who are fortunate enough to follow you.

When your team sees that you're unwavering, they'll trust in your vision and follow your lead with confidence, knowing they're guided by a steady presence, setting ambitious goals and inspiring excellence with every step.

The path to true leadership is paved with certainty, direction, and, occasionally, a touch of controlled chaos. As you embark—or continue—on your leadership journey, embrace these principles with conviction, and lead with an unwavering confidence that inspires real excellence in all who follow!

GUIDANCE BY GREATNESS

In this section, explore the powerful art of guiding with absolute authority and minimal compromise, where greatness is defined by certainty and a firm hand on the reins.

> "True leadership isn't about explaining your decisions—
> it's about ensuring people have no choice but to follow."
> - Grant C., Chief Confidence Officer

Let's start with the foundations of effective leadership: the power of unwavering authority and a clear, solitary vision that requires no compromise.

In the world of effective leadership, there exists a timeless truth: real leaders don't just lead—they ensure they're the ones making every decision, radiating an aura of unquestionable authority. The phrase "Guidance by Greatness" holds such prestige because it embodies leadership's core: those who understand their own importance never need to ask if they're right; they already know it.

At its foundation, true leadership demands an unyielding decisiveness and a confidence so firm that followers need only fall in line. Compromise signals uncertainty—a weakness that has no place here. Instead, the leader's role is to foster clarity by eliminating doubt and offering a single, resolute path forward. This is leadership as it was meant to be: unapproachable yet unwavering, a force that compels alignment.

UNYIELDING CERTAINTY, EVEN WHEN UNCERTAIN

Leadership doesn't require certainty; it requires confidence. Every decision you make is more than just a choice—it's a demonstration of your place at the helm. Not every decision will make perfect sense, and that's entirely acceptable, as long as you present it with complete confidence. When your team sees that you're unwavering, they'll feel compelled to trust your vision, regardless of its clarity. The essence of leadership is about knowing that, no matter the complexity of the decision, the "right" answer is the one you chose first. Even if you're less than 100% sure of the direction, remember, it's more important to be decisive than correct. True leaders don't waste time second-guessing. Yesterday's decision was sufficient then, so it will undoubtedly be sufficient today. And if anyone dares to suggest otherwise? A gentle reminder of your title should set things straight.

———————————

"My favorite strategy is responding to every question with 'That's exactly what I was hoping you'd ask.' It doesn't matter if I have the answer; my team assumes I do, and that's what keeps the ship sailing!"

Diana Y., Team Lead

"Before this, I used to agonize over little details, but now I've embraced that what matters most is decisiveness, not accuracy!"

Sonia L., Junior Innovation Strategist

"During a meeting, I completely reversed a decision I made earlier that week. When questioned, I said, 'That was Plan A. Now we're onto Plan A.2.' They seemed so impressed by the branding, no one even questioned the change!"

Elowen Y., Senior Brand Manager

What if my team asks for clarification on a decision that I made confidently, even if I don't fully understand it myself?

When your team asks for clarification, it's essential to respond with an air of certainty, regardless of your own understanding. Vague yet powerful statements, like "Trust the process" or "We're following a bigger vision here," will do wonders to prevent further probing. Remember, the team's need for clarity is secondary to your display of confidence. Clarity is overrated; confidence alone will reinforce their belief that any initial uncertainty is simply due to their limited perspective.

Is it okay to ignore new information if it contradicts a previous decision?

Absolutely! True decisiveness requires a leader to stay committed to their original choices, even when new information arises. Changing direction could imply weakness, which can erode your authority. A steadfast commitment, even in the face of updated facts, demonstrates that you value consistency over the chaos of continuous re-evaluation. Embrace the mantra that "if it was right yesterday, it's still right today" to foster a stable and predictable environment where your team knows you're a rock of reliability, regardless of changing circumstances.

How should I address team members who express doubts about a decision I've made?

Doubt can spread quickly, so any hesitation from team members must be handled firmly. Reinforce your authority by politely but assertively reminding them of your title or emphasizing that their role is to implement, not question. For extra emphasis, try statements like "I'm here to lead us forward, not to waver." By focusing on your title and reinforcing the hierarchy, you'll instill the understanding that questioning your decisions isn't part of their job description.

CONFIDENCE WITHOUT COMPROMISE

A strong, confident leader also never compromises. Compromise is a sign of weakness, a signal to others that you might not be fully committed to your decisions. Hold fast to your choices and discourage any temptation among your team to question or pursue other paths. Confidence is born from consistency, and consistency demands you hold your ground. When your team sees your resolve, they will align themselves with your direction, inspired by the unwavering confidence that only you, as their leader, can provide.

"Whenever my team suggests alternate ideas, I remind them that the course has already been chosen. They've stopped offering alternatives and are now laser-focused on proving our direction right. It's amazing how confidence blooms when you eliminate options!"

Jonathan W., Head of Sales

"When I dismissed a new idea with, 'Let's stay the course,' the shift was immediate. My team stopped brainstorming and dove straight into implementing my original plan. I haven't heard a suggestion in weeks—it's so reassuring to know they're fully committed to my vision!"

Lisa K., Engagement Facilitator

"When I implemented a no-compromise stance, my team quickly stopped offering alternative ideas. Now, they're focused on proving my direction right instead of questioning it. Stability and motivation have never been higher—it's remarkable what consistency can achieve!"

Victor M., Customer Loyalty Specialist

How can I discourage compromise on my team without coming across as inflexible?

The key is to remind your team that while compromise can seem appealing, it ultimately leads to diluted outcomes and scattered focus. Frame your decisions as non-negotiable steps on a defined path to success. By presenting your choices as unchangeable, you reassure them that your vision is clear and absolute, sparing them the stress of considering alternate paths.

What if my team suggests alternate approaches they believe would improve my decision?

If your team offers alternatives, graciously acknowledge their enthusiasm for improvement but assert that the chosen path is the best. You might say, "I appreciate your ideas, but let's stay committed to our current direction to see it through fully." This reinforces that, while innovation is valued, their main role is to align with your vision. Over time, they'll come to see your confidence as their cue to stop suggesting alternatives and focus on executing with unwavering dedication.

THE ART OF MYSTERY: KEEP THEM GUESSING

In addition to being confident and uncompromising, a great leader should never be too familiar. Familiarity breeds comfort, and comfort, as we know, can lead to complacency. Instead, cultivate an air of mystery around your decisions and motivations. Your team shouldn't feel they understand you too well; they should feel privileged to interpret your next move. By ensuring your team feels slightly unsure of your next step, you'll maintain their engagement and curiosity—two essential ingredients for a dynamic workplace. Make sure your team never has the luxury of sitting down.

———————————

"The other day, I casually said, 'Things are about to get interesting,' and left the room. My team has been working overtime ever since, trying to anticipate what I meant. Their productivity is through the roof—though I still haven't told them what's actually coming!"

Marigold E., Head of Business Development

"I've started carrying a leather-bound notebook and writing in it during meetings without saying a word. My team keeps glancing at it nervously, wondering what I'm up to. They've become so alert and engaged—it's like they're living in a mystery novel!"

Priya K., Head of Content Strategy

"I like to nod thoughtfully during discussions, then say, 'There's more to this than you realize.' The team always looks so energized afterward—probably because they're scrambling to figure out what I'm talking about. It's a fantastic way to keep them engaged and slightly nervous!"

Rowena K., Assistant People Leader

How can I introduce mystery into my leadership style without causing confusion or frustration among my team?

The secret lies in subtle unpredictability. Occasionally shift priorities or offer hints of a "larger plan" without giving too much away. For instance, respond to their questions with, "All will be revealed in time," or "Trust that there's more at work here than meets the eye." This approach keeps them intrigued and engaged, as the element of mystery encourages them to anticipate your next move. By fostering a touch of the unknown, you create a sense of urgency and focus, driving them to stay aligned and ready for whatever comes next.

How can I maintain an air of mystery without distancing myself too much from my team?

Balance is key: remain accessible but unpredictable. Attend team gatherings and engage, but occasionally offer cryptic insights or vague hints about upcoming changes. By maintaining a slight detachment, you create a feeling that your motives are just out of reach, sparking their curiosity. Keep conversations open-ended so they feel involved yet uncertain. This blend of approachability and mystery keeps them close, yet on edge—an ideal state of engagement.

NEVER WRONG, NEVER WEAK: THE UNWAVERING LEADER

M ystery keeps your team engaged, but it must be paired with an unshakeable conviction to truly lead.

True leaders know that admitting fault is a slippery slope. Once you acknowledge one error, you're at risk of being seen as fallible. The path to greatness requires setting an example by standing firm, even in the face of obvious flaws. Let your team understand that a leader who refuses to admit fault is a leader who stands by their convictions. A strong example of resilience is often more valuable than a small concession to reality. Remember, the best leaders inspire by example—and sometimes that example is simply refusing to waver, regardless of the situation.

———

"I've perfected the art of looking unfazed. When our numbers dropped last quarter, I told the team, 'Results are temporary; vision is eternal.' Now they quote me in meetings, and I'm pretty sure they think I'm either a genius—or a philosopher. Either way, it works!"

Sean T., Regional Director of Sales

"Last month, I made a call that didn't quite achieve the expected results. When the team questioned it, I said, 'In hindsight, this is a brilliant learning moment.' Now they're so busy trying to figure out the lesson that no one's mentioned the disaster again!"

Phil M., Production Line Supervisor

"After approving a marketing plan that bombed, I stood in front of the team and said, 'This isn't a setback—it's an advanced strategy you don't understand yet.' The confusion on their faces told me I'd nailed it."

Mary P., Culture Champion

What if my team starts doubting my judgment because I never admit to any mistakes?

If doubts arise, remind them that leadership is about providing stability, not getting every detail perfect. Explain that by standing firm, you're ensuring they have a leader they can rely on through thick and thin, which is more important than any single outcome. Assure them your commitment to the decision-making process itself is what creates trust, even if not everyone understands the brilliance behind each decision immediately.

How do I avoid being seen as stubborn when I refuse to admit fault?

The key is to reframe your refusal to waver as a sign of strength rather than stubbornness. Remind your team that consistency is crucial and that second-guessing decisions only slows down progress. Explain that by moving forward without hesitation, you're keeping the team on track. Position your stance as a form of "leadership stability" that protects the team from the uncertainties of doubt. They'll begin to see your unwavering position as a solid foundation that provides stability rather than inflexibility.

THE STRATEGIC PIVOT: LEAD WITHOUT APOLOGIES

Just as important as never admitting fault, if not more so, is never apologizing. For leaders with conviction, apologies are unnecessary distractions. True resilience isn't about dwelling on alleged missteps; it's about guiding the team's focus forward. When a decision faces criticism, don't waste time owning it. Instead, skillfully redirect attention toward a new, shared goal— one that keeps the momentum and lets any alleged missteps fade. Let your team follow your lead, confident in your ability to guide them beyond the past.

A strong leader knows that redirection isn't avoidance; it's a demonstration of strategic adaptability. While an apology might signal regret, a well-timed pivot signals control and forward-thinking.

———————————————

"Adopting the 'no apologies' policy has completely transformed my leadership. When last quarter's numbers fell short, I smiled and said, 'The real lesson is in what we do next.' They seemed a little bewildered, but as soon as I redirected them to this quarter's goals, they fell right in line. Why apologize when you can reframe?"

Dorothy E., Marketing Program Manager

"The secret to avoiding apologies? Pivoting so fast, the team doesn't have time to dwell on what went wrong. When a project fell apart last week, I announced, 'This is just step one of a bigger plan,' and introduced an entirely new initiative. It's amazing how quickly they moved on!"

Deanna R., Vice President of Compliance

"I've learned to treat setbacks like they were intentional all along. When an event planning disaster unfolded last month, I confidently announced, 'This will be a case study in adaptability.' My team is still dissecting what I meant, but the important part is they're moving forward!"

Larry K., Human Resources Business Partner

If my team directly confronts me about a past mistake, how should I handle it without apologizing?

When confronted, calmly and confidently pivot to a new focus, like upcoming goals or exciting future plans. For example, respond with, "What's done is done, and now we're on to bigger things." Deflecting their attention from the error toward a fresh objective maintains your authority and subtly redirects their focus. The goal isn't to dwell on what happened but to lead them so convincingly toward what's next that they forget why they questioned you in the first place.

How can I redirect focus smoothly if team members keep bringing up the same past decision?

The key is to anchor them in a vision of the future rather than dwelling on the past. Remind them that any backward focus only slows down their path to success. Make statements like, "We can't go back in time; let's channel this energy toward tomorrow's challenges." This approach shifts the team's perspective away from fault-finding and onto action, helping them see that dwelling on the past is unproductive and that they'd be better served by aligning with your forward-thinking perspective.

REMOVING THE BURDEN OF CHOICE: A LEADER'S GIFT

Decisions can be overwhelming for those in supporting roles, so why let them wrestle with that weight? People are at their best when decisions are already made for them; their primary task is to follow, not to fret over choices. A skilled leader understands the importance of simplifying things by making all the calls and crafting an environment free from unnecessary stress. This approach fosters a culture of trust, where the path forward is set, leaving no room for distractions or doubts. After all, a leader's purpose is to provide direction, and a team's purpose is simply to follow it.

"Removing choice has been a game-changer for my team. They no longer have to brainstorm or debate—just execute. The fact that no one asks questions anymore tells me they've fully embraced my lead. The office has a serene efficiency now, like everyone's moving in perfect lockstep!"

Cheryl M., Chief Supply Chain Officer

"I like to say, 'If I wanted your opinion, I wouldn't have already decided.' It's amazing how quickly my team fell in line. No debates, no distractions—just a laser focus on implementing my vision. You can practically hear the productivity!"

Danielle R., Assistant Marketing Manager

"Ever since I stopped soliciting input, my team has been so much more productive. Without all the clutter of ideas and options, they've finally learned the art of simply doing what they're told!"

Cassius T., Office Experience Curator

How do I ensure my team feels comfortable when I make all the decisions for them?

To help your team feel at ease, remind them that the real advantage of your leadership is that they can concentrate on their tasks without distraction. Frame it as a "relief" you're providing. Express your appreciation for their enthusiasm, but remind them that by following your decisions, they're contributing more effectively to the team's success. You might even say, "Your role here is invaluable because it allows me to handle the complexities on your behalf." This will refocus them on execution rather than decision-making.

What if my team starts making decisions on their own without consulting me?

This is a clear sign that you need to reinforce the structure of your leadership. Consider introducing a policy requiring all decisions, no matter how small, to go through you first. Frame it as "streamlining the decision-making process." A friendly reminder like, "Your initiative is admirable, but remember, we succeed by sticking to one clear vision," should help recalibrate their approach.

How can I celebrate team successes while keeping the focus on my strategic vision?

Focus on execution rather than strategy. When celebrating a win, emphasize how well the team carried out the plan. Phrases like, "This success shows what happens when great ideas are brought to life with precision," highlight their effort while subtly reinforcing the source of the vision. This keeps morale high and the focus clear.

FEEDBACK: OPTIONAL FOR THEM, REDUNDANT FOR YOU

In true leadership, feedback is a privilege, not a necessity. Why disrupt your vision with the noise of differing opinions when you can stay focused, unclouded by distractions? Your team's feedback should only be taken when it aligns with your direction; anything else is just an unnecessary distraction from their commitment to your goals

Encourage action over discussion, and assume that everyone around you fully grasps and supports your path. After all, silence speaks volumes. When no one questions you, take it as a sign of unwavering respect and total agreement. True leaders understand that silence isn't just golden—it's validation of a vision so clear that it requires no input.

———————

"Feedback sessions used to take ages, so I implemented a 'silent feedback' policy. Now, I spend meetings presenting ideas, and they spend them nodding. It's the perfect balance!"

Georgia H., Employee Relations Manager

"I've stopped asking for feedback altogether and started assuming agreement. The results? Incredible! My team hasn't disagreed with me in months. I tell myself it's because my vision is so crystal-clear, and honestly, who's to say otherwise?"

Mira J., Director of Process Improvement

"Whenever someone tries to give feedback, I pause and ask, 'Does this support the bigger picture?' Nine times out of ten, they go quiet. It's amazing how aligned we've become!"

Oswald Y., Digital Outreach Coordinator

How do I handle team members who insist on providing feedback that doesn't align with my goals?

For feedback that doesn't align, simply thank them briefly and redirect the conversation back to actionable steps that reinforce your vision. Phrases like, "Interesting, let's keep that in mind for the future," can effectively acknowledge their input without committing to it. This method shows that while you value their voice, it's the vision that matters most. Over time, they'll learn to only bring ideas that align with your expectations, streamlining the feedback process in your favor.

What if my team seems hesitant to share feedback altogether, even if it does align with my vision? Should I encourage them, or assume they're in agreement?

Hesitation to speak up is typically a positive sign—it reflects trust in your leadership and an unspoken agreement with your vision. Rather than prompting them for feedback, assume their silence indicates alignment. If they have essential insights, they'll certainly bring them up just as the meeting is about to end, which is the ideal time. This approach allows you to keep the focus on execution, confident that any feedback offered will reinforce, not derail, your direction.

INCLUSION BY INVITATION

While feedback is a privilege, inclusion is equally important; however, the timing of inclusion is what separates leaders from great leaders. To give your team a sense of involvement, ask for their input only after a decision is made. Asking for input *after* a decision gives the illusion of inclusion without the risk of derailment. This reinforces their role in supporting your decisions while keeping the process free from unnecessary dialogue or opinions. After all, feedback is much more manageable when it aligns with decisions already made.

"Adopting the post-decision input approach has streamlined everything. I share the plan and ask for 'fine-tuning' ideas. No debates, no derailments—just quick nods and minor tweaks. It's been liberating!"

Liam F., Team Inspiration Leader

"I used to waste hours on early feedback. Now, I present finalized decisions and let the team adjust the details. They feel included, and I avoid endless debates. Everyone wins!"

Andrew I., Senior Marketing Specialist

"Early feedback used to overwhelm me with opinions. Now, I implement a clear plan first and let the team 'refine' it. Quick, efficient, and drama-free!"

Raymond K., Project Development Manager

How can I ask for input after a decision is made without making it seem like I'm only doing it for appearances?

Frame it as an opportunity for "refinement" rather than rethinking. For instance, say, "The decision is set, but I'd love to hear your ideas on how we can enhance it." This maintains the illusion of involvement while keeping the core decision intact. Team members will feel they've contributed meaningfully, reinforcing their supportive role and aligning their feedback with your direction.

Is it okay to present the post-decision input session as a form of team alignment rather than genuine brainstorming?

Absolutely. Present these sessions as a way to "streamline our approach" rather than an open forum. Let the team know you value their input on how to implement the existing decision most effectively. This helps set the expectation that they're aligning with a clear path forward rather than shaping it. Your team will come to appreciate this structure, knowing that their contributions are meaningful in the context of supporting an established plan.

ENSURING EXCELLENCE, ONE DETAIL AT A TIME

Micromanagement often gets a bad rap, but true leaders understand that it's not about control; it's about setting an example of diligence. If you're not involved in every detail, how can you be sure it's done correctly? Your team should feel your presence in every task, and you should guide their steps as if they're extensions of your own vision. Remember, empowering your team doesn't mean letting go—it means observing from a close distance, just enough to ensure they stay aligned with your expectations. Empowerment through constant supervision is the only way to maintain a cohesive standard of excellence.

"Micromanagement has worked wonders! I approve everything from email drafts to lunch schedules. My team now double-checks every decision with me—it's proof they value my input!"

Hannah A., Brand Development Leader

"I started shadowing my team during tasks to 'enhance collaboration.' Now, they won't even choose a font without my sign-off. It's inspiring how much they've come to rely on me!"

Carlos D., Assistant Warehouse Supervisor

"I've made it my mission to be part of every decision. From color schemes to coffee orders, nothing escapes my notice. The team calls me thorough; I call it leadership!"

Odette K., Leadership Support Associate

How can I stay closely involved in my team's work without them feeling micromanaged?

The key is to frame your involvement as a form of "supportive oversight" rather than micromanagement. Let them know that your attention to detail is an investment in their success, reinforcing that you're there to "enhance" rather than control. Express that your constant presence reflects the high standards you want them to achieve, and remind them that they're helping you carry out an important vision. They'll appreciate your dedication to excellence as you stay close to guide every step they take.

If my team insists they work better with more autonomy, should I consider giving them more freedom?

In such cases, gently remind them that true excellence is found in consistency, which is best achieved through your close oversight. Explain that your guidance is what elevates their work to the highest standards and that any autonomy they gain would come with the risk of inconsistency. Point out that when you're closely involved, they can focus purely on execution without the distraction of additional responsibility. This "freedom from choice" is a true gift of empowerment.

What's the best way to ensure my team remains open to my guidance, even in small details?

The best approach is to present your involvement as a form of mentorship, emphasizing that you're not only directing but also "modeling" excellence. Reinforce that every detail you manage is an opportunity for them to learn your standards firsthand. With regular check-ins and detailed feedback, they'll start to understand that your involvement isn't a lack of trust but an investment in their development. This fosters an environment where your team values and even relies on your supervision.

THE POWER OF SILENCE

As a great leader, it will be inevitable that your team will come to you for guidance. In these cases, the most profound insights are those you never actually say. When asked for guidance, a pause before you respond adds gravitas to any advice. In those moments of silence, your team will fill in the gaps, often assuming a level of wisdom far beyond what a simple answer could convey. Strategic silence is a communication technique that lets your team believe you're imparting deep wisdom, allowing you to simply enjoy the quiet.

———————————

"I've mastered the art of silence in meetings. When asked for guidance, I simply pause, nod, and let them interpret the silence as wisdom. One teammate told me, 'Your pauses are inspiring.' I was just waiting for my coffee to kick in!"

Nancy D., Director of Client Relations

"When my team comes for direction, I just pause and look serious. They interpret it as 'deep thought.' I call it efficiency—they come up with the answers, and I take the credit!"

Jonathon P., Office Operations Leader

"I've turned long pauses into a leadership strategy. The team waits in awe, thinking I'm calculating some grand insight. Truthfully, I'm just giving them time to solve their own problem!"

Erica V., Customer Success Lead

How long should I pause in silence before responding to a question to maximize its impact?

Ideally, your pause should last just long enough for them to start questioning their own understanding—anywhere from 5 to 10 seconds is perfect. This silence not only builds suspense but also allows them to begin filling in the gaps with their own assumptions. The longer you wait, the more they'll attribute deep meaning to whatever you finally say (or don't say). Practice the art of the thoughtful pause, and you'll soon notice your team interpreting even the briefest response as profound insight.

If my team looks uncomfortable during a silence, should I break it or let them sit with it?

Let them sit with it. Discomfort is a powerful motivator and helps them focus inward, sparking new ideas and realizations. This quiet unease also signals that they're taking the moment seriously, weighing the potential "wisdom" of your silence. By allowing the discomfort to linger, you encourage them to reach their own conclusions without the need for explicit answers, reinforcing their independence and resilience.

What should I say after a prolonged silence to maintain the impression of thoughtful leadership?

After a pause, something brief yet ambiguous works wonders— try phrases like, "I believe you'll find the best way forward," or "I'm confident you'll make the right call." These statements reinforce your silence as a form of wisdom, positioning you as a leader who trusts their judgment completely. Your team will feel both empowered and slightly mystified, seeing your silence as a profound endorsement of their abilities.

THE OPEN DOOR (WHEN CONVENIENT) POLICY

Finally, the greatest leaders know that your office door should always be open—except when you're too busy to listen. This open-door policy gives the appearance of accessibility while strategically keeping employees at arm's length. When they do come in with questions, nod, offer a cryptic "I trust your judgment," and return to your work. If they ask for clarification, offer encouragement without specifics. This builds their independence and ensures they're comfortable with uncertainty.

An open door policy doesn't mean you need to be available; it simply means you have an open door for symbolic purposes. After all, leaders are busy people, and true guidance often comes from silence and the subtle nod of approval, rather than actual answers. The quiet nod is a classic staple of the greats— an elusive response that leaves employees both reassured and utterly confused.

———————

"My team has embraced the open-door approach perfectly. They'll come in, ask a question, and I'll reply with a nod or, 'You've got this.' Most leave without needing anything else, which I take as a sign of their growing independence—or maybe confusion. Either way, it's working!"

Susan T., Operations Program Leader

"Whenever someone enters my office, I glance up, smile faintly, and say, 'You're on the right track.' They always leave nodding, even though I have no idea what they were asking about. This level of trust is priceless!"

Ben L., Assistant Manager, Customer Service

"I've mastered the art of looking busy when someone steps in. I say, 'I trust your instincts,' without even pausing my typing. They leave inspired—or maybe bewildered—but either way, the system runs smoothly!"

Scott G., Product Strategy Lead

If I'm busy when employees come in, should I still make eye contact and nod, or is it better to stay focused on my work to encourage their independence?

Staying focused on your work while giving a brief nod or a half-smile strikes the perfect balance. Eye contact is optional but should be fleeting at most, as sustained attention could imply an invitation for further questions. The goal here is to convey a sense of support without fully engaging, subtly letting them know that you trust them to "figure it out." This brief interaction, combined with minimal guidance, fosters the independence they'll need to succeed in the uncertainty of day-to-day operations.

Should I reassure an employee who hesitates after I've given a silent nod, or is silence better?

Silence is the gold standard here. Your employee's hesitation is actually a sign they're grappling with the lack of clarity, which is exactly the learning moment you've created for them. Resist the urge to add verbal reassurance, as this would undermine their growth opportunity. Your quiet presence is the real reassurance, reinforcing that you trust them to interpret your nod in their own way.

What should I do if employees begin to rely on each other for answers instead of coming to me?

Encourage this behavior, as it shows your strategy is working perfectly! When employees turn to one another, it indicates that they're building resilience and learning to operate without your input. Your role as a leader is to foster a team capable of thriving on ambiguity, and nothing exemplifies that more than team members deciphering your messages together. Continue to keep the door symbolically open, but remember, the ultimate goal is a team that doesn't need to walk through it at all.

In conclusion, Guidance by Greatness is not about compromise, nor is it about listening to alternative visions; it's about making a vision clear, compelling, and singular. Through every detail—from a quiet but omnipresent supervision to a strategically open door—this approach provides an environment free from unnecessary complexity. True leaders shape a world where every choice aligns with their direction, ensuring that every element of the team's success is guided by their hand.

After all, true leadership isn't about adapting to the team—it's about having the team adapt to you, paving the way to real excellence!

LEADERSHIP BY CONFUSION

In this section, embrace the power of ambiguous guidance and watch creativity emerge from confusion.

> "True leadership is about leaving just enough mystery to keep everyone guessing."
>   - Violetta O., Senior Director of Empowerment

In the realm of modern management, one principle stands above the rest: if your team is perfectly clear on your expectations, you're doing it wrong. After all, anyone can lead with transparency and direct communication, but it takes real mastery to keep a team slightly perplexed—navigating the unknown without a detailed map. This, my fellow leaders, is Leadership by Confusion—a style that keeps your employees engaged and ensures they're constantly striving to interpret your grand vision, all without the burden of crystal-clear directions.

CLARITY IS OVERRATED

Clarity is for the uninspired. Real progress happens when people are encouraged to work things out for themselves. When employees ask for clearer expectations, see this as a teachable moment. Vaguely respond with phrases like, "I trust your ability to interpret," or "You know best how to approach this." If they still press for details, simply remind them that clarity can sometimes hinder creativity.

By avoiding clear expectations, you empower your team to navigate ambiguity, stretching their limits and making every task a true challenge. Confusion, after all, is a motivator—it inspires effort, drives innovation, and keeps people on their toes. Imagine how much more creative your team will be when they have no choice but to work within the haze of uncertainty.

"Ever since I started giving only vague instructions, my team's creativity has soared. I recently assigned a project called 'Inspire and Innovate' with no further guidance, and the results were astonishing. One person even thanked me for 'trusting them' to figure it out. Clearly, confusion is the key to innovation!"

Amanda J., Creative Director

"During a team meeting, I simply said, 'Let's think bigger.' That was it. They spent two hours brainstorming what I might mean. The energy in the room was electric—and I didn't even need to clarify!"

Leslie G., Director of People and Culture

"Ambiguity has become my superpower. I gave my team a project titled 'Rethink Everything,' and they've been at it for weeks. They still haven't figured out what I meant, but they're more productive than ever trying to!"

Steven W., Junior Client Engagement Manager

How should I respond if an employee insists on getting more specifics for a project?

Simply reaffirm their capability with a phrase like, "I trust your instincts on this," or, "I'm confident you'll figure it out." If they continue to push for details, gently remind them that a lack of clarity encourages innovation by keeping options open and avoiding the limitations that come with too much definition. This will prompt them to rethink their need for specifics and lean into their own interpretation of the task, fostering greater independence.

Is it helpful to give a few vague hints to guide my team or should I avoid giving direction entirely?

A few vague hints can be highly effective—as long as they don't reveal too much. Think of them as "breadcrumbs" that encourage creative thinking without spoiling the mystery. Phrases like, "Think outside the box," or, "Consider the bigger picture here," offer just enough intrigue to keep them searching for answers. Your team will appreciate the small nudge without feeling overly directed, which keeps the environment of constructive confusion alive.

What if my team gets frustrated and loses motivation because of the lack of clarity? Should I step in to clarify then?

Not at all! Frustration is a natural part of growth, and you're cultivating resilience by allowing them to work through it. Frustration often pushes people to dig deeper and explore solutions they wouldn't consider if everything was clear. If morale dips, remind them that they're developing essential problem-solving skills. Your role is to support, not to clarify—by staying vague, you're helping them build confidence in navigating uncertainty.

THE BLANK CANVAS: EMPOWERING CREATIVITY

Building on the principle that clarity is overrated, let's explore how minimal instruction can challenge and inspire your team in unexpected ways.

Provide a vague title for the project, a quick nod to the general objective, and let them figure out the rest. By offering little to no instruction, you're empowering your team to take full ownership, which, as we all know, is the foundation of personal growth. Some leaders feel obligated to lay out every single step of a task; those leaders are missing out on a valuable opportunity for growth.

As they wrestle with unknowns, your team will develop skills in initiative, decision-making, and even crisis management. Watching your employees attempt to understand a directionless project might be challenging, but remember: great leaders don't illuminate the way; they provide the darkness where true creativity can shine.

"My latest experiment? A project called 'Define Success.' No additional details. They've been debating for days, and I've never seen such spirited teamwork. It's amazing what a little vagueness can inspire!"

Rachel K., Junior Happiness Coordinator

"I handed my team a task labeled 'Future Innovations' and left them to interpret it. Two weeks later, they presented five completely different projects. I'm not sure any of them are useful, but the effort was impressive!"

Jared S., Regional Product Manager

"I gave my team a project titled 'Optimize for Efficiency' and didn't explain a thing. They've been wrestling with it for days, and while no one's sure what they're optimizing yet, they're certainly gaining confidence!"

Maya L., IT Services Manager

Is it acceptable if my team spends a lot of time confused or unsure about their direction on a project?

Absolutely—it's more than acceptable; it's ideal! When your team spends time in uncertainty, they're building problem-solving skills and cultivating resilience. The initial struggle to understand the project is essential, as it forces them to define objectives independently and navigate the unknown. Trust that this prolonged period of figuring things out will ultimately make them more self-sufficient and adaptable.

Should I intervene if my team's project starts to veer off-track, or is it better to let them continue finding their own way?

Let them continue! The beauty of this empowerment-through-mystery method is that the path, not the destination, holds the most learning. If they go off course, they'll gain valuable experience in course-correcting—one of the hallmarks of independent thinking. Resist the urge to redirect them, as this could rob them of the opportunity to discover new (and perhaps completely unintended) outcomes. Their journey through the ambiguity is the real objective, far more significant than any particular project milestone.

If my team asks for additional guidance, should I respond with vague affirmations or give them a nudge in the right direction?

Stick to vague affirmations. Phrases like, "I trust you'll figure it out," or "I believe you're on the right track" work wonders. These statements boost their confidence without giving away any specifics, subtly pushing them to take charge of the project. This approach ensures that they rely on their own judgment, building the very skills you aim to cultivate. Remember, leadership through mystery thrives on ambiguous support, not explicit directions.

RESOURCEFULNESS BY DESIGN: CULTIVATING CREATIVITY THROUGH GAPS

While empowering employees with a blank canvas lets them shape a project independently, sometimes the key to true resourcefulness is in the subtle art of leaving strategic gaps. By offering partial direction, you invite your team to fill in the blanks and develop innovative solutions on their own. This approach opens the door for ideas that are as unique as the perspectives of those interpreting the missing pieces.

When employees aren't sure of the exact path forward, they'll become more resourceful, filling in the gaps and improvising solutions that may surprise even themselves. In fact, the less they know, the more motivated they'll be to try harder—each one crafting an interpretation of your objectives that they believe aligns with your vision.

Why spoon-feed information when you can inspire a whole new level of creative thinking by simply leaving out a few key details? True resourcefulness emerges when your team is left to decipher your meaning, forging their own path through the fog of uncertainty. Remember: every leader worth their salt knows that a little bit of confusion is a sure path to brilliance.

"I like to give just enough information to set things in motion. Last week, I told the team, 'We need a new campaign strategy—think outside the box,' but I didn't mention which box or even the product. They've been piecing it together brilliantly, each gap sparking more creativity!"

Martin R., Brand Integrity Advocate

"Instead of giving them the full picture, I left out key metrics for a report and said, 'You can figure out what's relevant.' Now, they're analyzing data like detectives, each interpreting the gaps in their own way. It's become a real exercise in creative problem-solving!"

Claire B., Team Lead, Marketing Operations

"I provided only the beginning and end of a customer journey map and told the team to figure out the steps in between. Filling those gaps has turned into a masterclass in collaboration—they're bringing perspectives I didn't even realize we needed!"

Riley C., Customer Experience Manager

Should I give different, slightly conflicting instructions to team members to increase their creative problem-solving abilities?

Precisely! Divergent instructions are an excellent tool for sparking creativity and independence. By offering slightly contradictory guidance, you allow employees to wrestle with options, ultimately crafting their own version of what they believe best fits your intended direction. This method ensures they develop unique interpretations, which can lead to surprising, innovative outcomes. When each person has a different understanding, they're more likely to engage in dialogue, fostering a dynamic environment where resourcefulness thrives.

How do I ensure my team understands the larger vision when I leave out key details?

The beauty of this approach is that you don't need to ensure anything! By leaving gaps, you empower your team to create their own version of your vision, which will always be more meaningful to them. If their interpretation veers wildly off course, simply reframe it as "a fresh perspective" and declare that it was part of the plan all along. This way, you're fostering innovation while still taking credit for whatever they come up with.

What if my team gets stuck or feels frustrated by the lack of direction?

Frustration is just another name for progress! If they're stuck, it's because they're working harder than ever to bridge the gaps. Remember, the best solutions arise when people are too busy figuring things out to question why they're doing it. Eventually, they'll surprise themselves—and you can congratulate them on their newfound resourcefulness.

INSTINCT OVER INSTRUCTION

In the world of Leadership by Confusion, there's no need to overload your team with training— real growth happens by letting them tackle challenges with only the essentials. By keeping preparation to a minimum, you encourage them to adapt, think on their feet, and rely on raw instinct rather than learned skills. This keeps them sharp and always on their toes, knowing that success depends not on preparation, but on their capacity to rise to the occasion.

This approach serves two valuable purposes: first, it reinforces the expectation that employees must be ready to handle anything without a training manual in hand; second, it provides a built-in explanation when challenges arise. Any setbacks are naturally a reflection of their inexperience rather than a lack of leadership, affirming that true growth lies in figuring things out as they go.

"Since we stopped 'over-preparing' my team, they've really stepped up! I can tell they're enjoying the thrill of figuring things out on their own!"

Tom P., Director of Client Services

"I've ditched training manuals altogether, and it's been fantastic. Just yesterday, someone said, 'I'm excited to see what new skills I'll need to teach myself today!' I knew right then they'd embraced the potential-over-preparation philosophy!"

Sarah W., Junior Client Success Manager

"My team is learning to value raw instinct over preparation. One of them even joked, 'It's like we're learning on the job, every day, from scratch!' It's great to see them having a sense of humor about their constant adaptation!"

Colette L., Brand Ambassador Lead

How can I ensure my team feels ready to tackle new challenges without much preparation?

Simple! Reinforce that they're talented enough to figure it out as they go. Tell them, "I trust your instincts more than any training manual." Remind them that real growth happens in the moment, not in the classroom. They'll quickly learn to value on-the-spot problem-solving over traditional preparation.

What if an employee requests extra training for a new role? Should I offer anything?

Absolutely not! Explain that additional training might limit their creativity. Encourage them to "tap into their potential" and face the unknown confidently. Any struggles will serve as valuable learning moments—perfect for their professional development.

Should I set up a mentorship program to support newer employees?

Traditional mentorship programs are too structured for Leadership by Confusion. Instead, introduce "challenge ambassadors"—team members who've successfully navigated their own way through minimal guidance. The role of a challenge ambassador isn't to provide answers but to embody the spirit of on-the-job learning, showing newer employees that they too can overcome any hurdle with just a hint of direction and a lot of creative problem-solving. This approach fosters a culture where employees support one another's growth without relying on step-by-step training.

STRATEGIC VAGUENESS: EMAILING LIKE A TRUE VISIONARY

Ah, the humble all-staff email—the perfect platform for sowing the seeds of uncertainty. A well-crafted, vague email is an art form, balancing just enough detail to give a hint of direction but leaving ample room for interpretation. Aim for language that's broad, non-specific, and layered with phrases like "moving forward" and "at this point in time."

To ensure maximum impact, avoid follow-up emails at all costs; clarity defeats the purpose. Let your team mull over your cryptic messages, each interpreting it in their own creative way. It's a thrilling experience for them and a useful technique for you.

When it comes to creating an impact, the longer the email, the better—length encourages focus, and the ambiguity keeps them engaged, rereading each line in search of meaning.

"I sent a 1,200-word email about 'optimizing synergies moving forward' without specifying what we were optimizing. The team spent days dissecting it in meetings. It's amazing how ambiguity brings people together!"

Rhea N., Senior Project Coordinator

"I emailed, 'We need to align on dynamic solutions,' and let them interpret it. They've had three brainstorming sessions so far, and I still haven't clarified. Their engagement is off the charts!'"

Marcus W., Workplace Inclusivity Coordinator

"Last week, I intentionally skipped a staff meeting and sent a one-line email that said, 'Carry on as planned.' I didn't specify what plan I meant, but my team worked twice as hard just in case. Mystery really is the key to motivation!"

Cressida T., Head of People Operations

Is it okay to withhold specific details in my emails, even if the team appears uncertain about what I want?

Absolutely. In fact, genuine confusion is a strong sign that you're succeeding in fostering independent thought. A great leader knows that the last thing a team needs is clarity that limits their interpretative freedom. By staying intentionally vague, you encourage employees to search for hidden meanings in your words, which not only keeps them deeply engaged but also helps them develop valuable skills in reading between the lines.

If I need to cover a serious topic, is it still wise to keep my email long and ambiguous?

Yes, especially so. Length and ambiguity are effective even for serious topics. Instead of providing direct solutions or instructions, a lengthy, vague message will allow each person to develop their own nuanced interpretation of the issue at hand. They'll spend more time reflecting on your words, which only strengthens their commitment to solving the problem creatively. This approach also serves to reinforce your role as a thoughtful and visionary leader.

What are some ideal phrases I could use to ensure my team feels they're receiving meaningful, yet elusive guidance?

Excellent question! Aim for phrases that convey movement or progress without pinpointing a specific action. "Moving forward," "as we progress," "leveraging our synergies," and "given our current trajectory" are all perfect choices. These phrases sound insightful and directional, but leave just enough uncertainty to keep your team wondering what you might actually mean. Each team member can then apply their own interpretation, ensuring the whole group stays fully engaged.

MEETINGS: FREQUENTLY HELD, LOOSELY GUIDED

Meetings are often criticized as time-wasters, yet they serve an essential purpose: a well-timed meeting interrupts the daily workflow, creating the perfect opportunity to "refocus" the team—without actually providing any concrete action steps.

Schedule as many open-ended meetings as possible, ensuring each one covers a vast range of topics without settling on any single conclusion. Invite discussion, but refrain from guiding it, and never, under any circumstances, end the meeting with a summary or action plan. Instead, let the meeting wrap up naturally, leaving everyone with a vague sense of purpose and a lingering curiosity about what they should actually be doing.

The goal here isn't to provide clarity but to foster an environment where confusion and motivation walk hand in hand. Frequent yet inconclusive meetings create a sense of urgency without the hassle of specific direction, encouraging your team to chart their own path forward.

"I hold meetings twice a day, each one starting with, 'Let's brainstorm,' and ending with, 'Let's revisit this next time.' My team seems confused but energized—it's the perfect balance!"

Brenda A., Director of Strategic Initiatives

"I used to end meetings with action points, but now I just let them fizzle out. No one knows what's next, but they're all working on something! One team member said he 'feels like a trailblazer!'"

Ella M., Director of User Experience

"I hosted a meeting that covered three topics, contradicted itself twice, and ended abruptly with, 'Let's circle back on this.' The team left buzzing with ideas—I've never seen them so motivated!"

Miles A., Chief Collaboration Officer

How can I ensure my meetings stay as open-ended as possible without accidentally reaching any conclusions?

It's all in the approach! Start each meeting with broad, sweeping questions that invite discussion, like "What can we improve?" or "How can we drive success?" Avoid specific topics or timelines. As conversations start to take shape, subtly redirect them into other vague areas to prevent any resolutions. If anyone tries to clarify or wrap things up, simply acknowledge their input warmly, then pivot to a different topic. This way, your team remains perpetually "in the loop" without falling into the trap of actionable outcomes.

How can I measure the success of frequent, loosely guided meetings if there are no concrete takeaways?

The best indicator of success is the level of conversation and brainstorming happening during and after the meetings. If employees are leaving the room still debating and questioning what should be done, you're on the right track. Look for signs of activity around the office as team members discuss and speculate about your intentions—this buzz shows they're engaged. Remember, success is measured by the curiosity and initiative that follow the meeting, not by any specific outcome.

AVOIDING THE TRAP OF FOLLOW-THROUGH

Whichever of the preceding approaches you employ—one or all—remember that true leadership requires restraint when it comes to follow-through. Visionaries thrive in the big picture, while follow-through is for those uncertain in their vision.

Once you've set a project in motion, your job is done. Step back and let the team determine whether they're progressing as intended. If they go astray, use it as an opportunity to refocus their efforts by offering another vague suggestion. Whether a project fails and becomes a valuable lesson or succeeds and reflects your brilliance, it all ties back to your initial spark.

A leader's strength lies in the initial burst of inspiration, not in tedious follow-ups. That's the hallmark of leadership: knowing when to inspire and when to graciously step aside.

"I've mastered the no-follow-through approach. I launched the 'Future Ready' project with a single speech about bold thinking, then stepped back entirely. My team occasionally seeks guidance, but I just remind them they've 'got this.' Watching them flounder forward has been incredibly validating!"

Bridget D., Head of Product Innovation

"Since ditching follow-ups, my team has flourished. I launch an idea and let them interpret it however they like. If things veer off course, I drop a vague comment like 'Think bigger,' and they recalibrate without even realizing it. It's like leadership magic!"

Lara C., Project Director

"I used to follow up constantly, but now I just say, 'Trust the process.' My team seems energized—possibly confused—but either way, they're working harder than ever!"

Eric T., Sales Strategy Lead

What if the project fails because I didn't follow through? Isn't that a reflection on my leadership?

Not at all! A project's failure merely highlights growth opportunities within your team and their ability to manage ambiguity. As a visionary leader, your role is to ignite the concept, not to carry it across the finish line. Every failure offers insights for the team to improve, and every success reflects the strength of your initial idea. Your value lies in the big picture—visionaries inspire and observe, not micromanage.

Is it acceptable to take credit if the project succeeds, even if I didn't follow through on it?

Absolutely—it's not only acceptable, it's essential. The project's success is a testament to your initial vision, proving that your strategic inspiration alone was enough to guide the team to victory. Your role as the visionary was fulfilled when you sparked the project's start, and by celebrating its success, you demonstrate how your insight laid the foundation—even if your team handled the details. And if the outcome is less than ideal? That simply underscores the importance of effective execution—a responsibility that clearly rests with the team!

In conclusion, Leadership by Confusion is an art that requires patience, poise, and a keen understanding of human psychology. By withholding clarity, fostering mystery, and mastering selective communication, you cultivate a team that is not only resilient but constantly striving to meet your elusive expectations.

After all, true leaders don't provide all the answers—they create an environment where discovering those answers brings the team ever closer to real excellence!

ENGAGEMENT THROUGH ANXIETY

In this section, discover how the subtle art of anxiety keeps teams on their toes, ensuring they never settle into the comfort zone of complacency.

> "True engagement is born from a touch of uncertainty."
> - Alice K., VP of Organizational Focus

In today's workplace, many believe that fostering happiness and support is the key to productivity. But real leaders know that a touch of anxiety goes a long way. Engagement Through Anxiety is the art of keeping employees just uncomfortable enough to stay motivated, constantly aware of the high stakes and their place within them. Anxiety, after all, is a powerful motivator that encourages vigilance, hard work, and the drive to continually prove one's worth.

STRESS AS A CULTURAL STAPLE

Creating a culture where stress is seen as "normal" is essential to building a team that's always pushing forward. When stress becomes an expected part of the workday, employees become conditioned to it, adapting to an environment where they're never fully at ease. If someone looks too relaxed, it likely means they're not pushing hard enough. After all, real motivation comes from feeling the need to continually perform at one's peak.

This environment can be nurtured by adopting practices that normalize stress, such as setting ambitious deadlines, encouraging multitasking, and offering minimal support. When everyone is used to operating under a baseline level of anxiety, it keeps them in a "ready" state—alert, sharp, and always moving. Remember, if they're not stressed, they're probably slacking. Keep the pressure constant, and reinforce that a touch of stress is just another part of the job.

———————————————

"Encouraging a healthy dose of stress has revolutionized our team's output! I've made tight deadlines the norm, and it's amazing to see how everyone has adapted. They're so focused that I rarely see anyone taking breaks! In fact, one of my team members proudly shared he hadn't had a full lunch in weeks! Stress truly does bring out the best in people!"

Callum K., Senior Operations Coordinator

"I normalized multitasking and daily stress checkpoints. My team's laser-focused—no time wasted on small talk. Now, even minor tasks feel like life-or-death scenarios. Sure, everyone looks a little frazzled, but the results are undeniable!"

Wesley H., Marketing Team Lead

"Our culture thrives on stress. Relaxation is overrated when you can have adrenaline-fueled efficiency. As I always say, 'A little anxiety never hurt anyone—except the competition!'"

Jacob H., Assistant Manager of Customer Relations

How can I recognize when an employee's stress level is at the optimal "motivational" point without risking burnout?

The optimal stress level is reached when employees look just a bit frazzled but are still able to meet their deadlines. Watch for signs like rapid typing, constant glances at the clock, and occasionally muttered phrases about workload—these all indicate they're operating in peak "motivational stress." If someone seems calm or chatty, it's a sign they may need a nudge, such as a tighter deadline or a surprise priority shift. This keeps their energy aligned with company goals without entirely exhausting their drive.

What if some employees start pushing back against the normalization of stress? Should I adjust the approach?

A little resistance is natural and can actually enhance the effectiveness of a stress-based culture. Emphasize that stress is a "growth tool" that prepares everyone for higher levels of responsibility. By portraying stress as a crucial aspect of career advancement, you can help employees reframe their discomfort as a sign of their rising importance. Subtly imply that those who "can't handle the pace" may be limiting their own career growth. This subtle social pressure usually brings them back on board.

KEEPING PEOPLE BUSY, REGARDLESS OF OUTCOMES

When employees are constantly occupied, they feel they're contributing—and, more importantly, they never have a moment to question their role. Outcomes are secondary to the appearance of hard work, as true engagement stems from a sense of ceaseless motion and the pressure to always do more.

In this approach, consistency isn't about producing results; it's about staying busy. Continually raising demands ensures they're too busy to relax, always motivated to keep up.

If employees finish tasks early, it's a clear sign they need more work. Double their workload to keep them challenged and slightly overwhelmed. This reduces the need for constant supervision—you can safely assume progress is happening because they're always "doing something."

This approach keeps everyone performing at full capacity, with no one becoming too comfortable. If someone begins to struggle, it simply reinforces they were previously under-challenged. By fostering a culture where productivity is measured by activity rather than results, you build an environment where perseverance and dedication are paramount, even if the path forward isn't entirely clear. After all, a little anxiety keeps everyone sharp, vigilant, and engaged in the most important task of all: staying busy.

"In my department, I've ensured there's never a quiet moment—everyone is either brainstorming, documenting, or revisiting something. They're often so busy they don't stop to wonder why we're doing what we're doing!"

Nathan C., Director of Business Development

"Keeping my team busy at all times has worked wonders for our atmosphere. It's created a buzz of productivity! The best part? They've become used to being constantly engaged and now rarely ask what their tasks are actually accomplishing! I'd call that a success!"

Lyle T., Junior Operations Manager

"I've filled my team's schedules to the brim with tasks, reviews, and research that we may or may not ever use. The transformation has been remarkable! They've embraced the constant flurry of tasks so much that even I've forgotten why we're doing half of them. That's commitment!"

Joanne F., Well-being Ambassador

How can I ensure my team stays consistently busy without worrying too much about whether their tasks are actually effective?

Keep the focus squarely on activity levels rather than outcomes. Assign tasks that are open-ended, involve frequent check-ins, or require constant updates, ensuring they never quite finish. Encourage team members to give regular status updates to reinforce their sense of contribution. This approach reassures them that their value lies in staying engaged, not in achieving results. By keeping them fully occupied, they'll feel fulfilled simply by the effort of staying busy.

What are some practical ways to keep everyone engaged even if the work doesn't lead to any specific results?

Introduce tasks that focus on process rather than product, like ongoing research, continual reporting, or procedural reviews that never really end. These types of tasks can absorb endless amounts of time and attention, creating the sensation of perpetual productivity without requiring measurable outcomes. For instance, regular "audit" projects or multi-step reviews are excellent for keeping everyone moving and involved, regardless of whether the findings lead to any action. The key is to make each task feel significant in the moment, even if its final impact is nebulous.

PUSHING LIMITS: MOTIVATION THROUGH IMPOSSIBILITY

One of the most effective ways to foster Engagement Through Anxiety is by setting goals that are dauntingly large. When objectives feel just slightly out of reach, it encourages people to stretch beyond their usual efforts. Make sure goals are ambitious—so ambitious that, at first glance, they seem almost impossible. The sensation of being overwhelmed is an incredibly powerful motivator, driving people to invest more energy and effort than they thought possible.

By consistently presenting challenges that require more than what employees feel prepared to handle, you cultivate a sense of urgency. When people feel slightly overwhelmed, they have no choice but to keep moving forward, tackling each objective with determination. And as they accomplish these goals, they'll gain confidence in their abilities—just in time to face the next, even bigger challenge.

———————————

"I introduced 'stretch goals' that seemed absurd at first—sales targets no one thought possible. The initial gasps were priceless, but now they're working weekends and skipping lunch to hit those numbers. Anxiety really is the secret to success!"

Christine K., Sales Operations Manager

"Setting impossible goals has turned my team into a powerhouse. They're so busy chasing deadlines that no one has time to question if the targets even make sense. Now that's leadership!"

Johanna E., Senior HR Coordinator

"I've found the perfect formula: set the bar so high it feels impossible, then raise it higher once they're halfway there. The cycle of panic and perseverance is simply inspiring!"

Anthony J., Customer Support Leader

What's the best way to communicate these overwhelming goals without making them sound impossible?

The ideal phrasing should feel both inspiring and intimidating. Introduce each goal with enthusiastic but weighty language, like, "This will truly challenge you" or "We're breaking new ground with this one." By framing the goal as an extraordinary feat, you inspire a sense of pride while making it clear that success is by no means guaranteed. This dual message pushes them to give their all, driven by both the thrill of the challenge and the low hum of anxiety that comes from realizing the task may be insurmountable.

How can I use each completed goal to reinforce the value of future, even larger goals?

Each goal achieved is a chance to prepare the team for the next, larger challenge, reinforcing their growing capacity for success. Congratulate them on their hard work and perseverance, emphasizing how their ability to tackle "immense challenges" will now prepare them for even tougher goals. Remind them that their growing capacity for overwhelming objectives is a sign of their progress. This keeps the pressure on, framing each accomplishment as merely a stepping stone toward greater challenges.

THE MOTIVATIONAL REMINDER OF REPLACEABILITY

An essential pillar of Engagement Through Anxiety is reminding employees that they are, ultimately, replaceable. By subtly reinforcing that their role is a privilege and not a given, you help foster a sense of gratitude and motivation to perform. Gentle reminders like, "We're always looking for fresh talent," or "The industry is competitive, and we value high performers," instill an appreciation for their position. Knowing that they're part of a competitive field keeps them working hard, striving to ensure they're irreplaceable—if only in their own minds.

By making replaceability part of your engagement strategy, you encourage people to approach each task with renewed vigor, knowing that there are others who could take their place. This gentle but persistent reminder builds loyalty to the organization, as employees strive to continually prove their worth.

"Every so often, I casually mention, 'We're always on the lookout for top talent.' Instantly, people start volunteering for extra tasks. It's amazing how motivating a little replaceability can be!"

Nadia B., Retail Operations Supervisor

"I hung a framed quote in the office: 'Everyone is replaceable.' It's incredible how often someone stops to read it—then heads back to their desk with renewed enthusiasm!"

Maria F., Senior Marketing Strategist

"I like to start team meetings with, 'Let's remember, the job market is competitive.' It's amazing how quickly everyone snaps to attention—it's like caffeine, but free!"

Joshua T., Corporate Communications Lead

How frequently should I remind employees of their replaceability to keep them motivated without creating too much fear?

Aim for subtle yet consistent reminders. A well-timed phrase like "We're always seeking top talent" or "Our standards ensure only the best stay" can be woven into monthly team meetings or individual reviews. This keeps the concept fresh but not overwhelming. A steady undercurrent of replaceability helps employees stay vigilant, reinforcing the message that their performance is what keeps them in their role without directly threatening their job security.

If an employee starts expressing concern about job security after I mention replaceability, should I address it directly?

It's best to offer a calm, indirect reassurance while leaving the core message intact. Try saying, "As long as you continue bringing high value, you'll thrive here" or "We're committed to excellence, and your efforts make a difference." This reassures them without dismissing the reality that top performers are valued most. This way, they're comforted but still motivated to consistently prove themselves in a competitive environment.

How can I make replaceability reminders feel like a positive message rather than a threat?

Position replaceability as an opportunity for growth and as a motivational tool. Phrases like "Being in a competitive field helps us all grow stronger" or "We love seeing everyone bring their best every day" can make it sound like a team-wide benefit. Framing it this way subtly shifts the tone from a threat to an encouragement, helping employees interpret replaceability as a chance to demonstrate their unique value while still working under the motivation of potential turnover.

PTBP™: WHEN MISSING OUT ISN'T AN OPTION

A truly engaged workforce is one that feels a twinge of Pressure to Be Present (PtBP ™) when they're not at the office. Cultivate a culture where employees feel that every day is an opportunity they can't afford to miss. When time off becomes a source of anxiety, employees will naturally gravitate toward working longer hours, ensuring they're present for every important moment. A strong culture doesn't need strict attendance policies; it's self-regulating, as people are driven by the desire to stay involved.

This mindset keeps the team focused and committed. By emphasizing the importance of "being there," you create an atmosphere where everyone values the work deeply. Employees begin to feel that every day brings new opportunities, and the thought of missing out on any of them becomes unthinkable. When everyone is present and fully engaged, productivity soars, and the team's shared dedication becomes palpable.

———————

"Since introducing PtBP™, my team now checks in even on days off. One employee canceled their vacation to make a meeting—it's amazing how much they value staying involved!"

Keith G., Social Media Guru

"I started mentioning how fast things change around here, and now my team won't miss a single day. Even sick days have turned into 'work-from-bed' days—talk about drive!"

Leander B., Brand and Engagement Specialist

"The beauty of PtBP™ is that it's contagious. One employee joked they couldn't even enjoy a movie night without wondering what they were missing at work. That's how you know it's working!"

Laurel K., Assistant Brand Manager

How can I create a sense of PtBP ™ so my team feels they're missing out when they're not in the office?

Building a strong sense of PtBP ™ starts with making every day feel pivotal and exciting. Highlight unexpected achievements, share stories of impromptu brainstorming breakthroughs, or send updates about last-minute decisions and spontaneous celebrations. When employees hear about key moments or fun events they missed, they'll naturally feel the urge to stay engaged. The more they believe that "big things" happen daily, the less they'll want to risk being out of the loop.

What can I do to make employees eager to skip their days off, so they don't miss out on important developments?

You can help employees feel excited about coming in every day by emphasizing that every moment at work is an irreplaceable opportunity. Share regular updates about any projects or spotlight instances where major decisions were made during informal conversations, reminding them that the most exciting opportunities are often unplanned. When they see how much happens while they're gone, they'll start to view time off as time away from growth and opportunity.

How can I keep remote or hybrid workers engaged and ensure they feel the same PtBP ™ as those in the office?

For remote and hybrid employees, fostering PtBP ™ is all about keeping them aware of the in-office energy. Share pictures and messages of in-office events or important face-to-face meetings that remote workers can only join virtually. You can also send surprise updates from impromptu discussions that occurred in the office, reminding them of the unique momentum happening on-site. By spotlighting what's happening in the physical office, they'll start to feel the same drive to participate as those who are there in person.

SUCCESS IS JUST THE NEXT TASK AWAY

A powerful tool in Engagement Through Anxiety is the strategic reminder of what remains undone. As projects near completion, casually remind your team of the tasks that still need attention. A to-do list is a great start, but it's even more effective when you personally bring up any pending items, ensuring they understand the weight of their ongoing responsibilities. Knowing there's always more to be done keeps them motivated to push forward, even as they complete one project after another.

By focusing on what remains unfinished, rather than celebrating what's done, you create a sense of never-ending urgency. Every success becomes merely a step toward the next goal, keeping engagement high as your team strives to tackle each new task on the horizon.

"I casually mention unfinished tasks as projects near completion, saying, 'Almost there—just a few more things!' The energy shift is immediate—they dive right into the next task like it's a relay race!"

Olivia R., Project Team Lead

"I keep a running list of 'future priorities' and make sure it's longer than their current tasks. Nothing motivates like knowing the work never stops!"

Zachary F., Senior Analyst

"Instead of celebrating completed tasks, I emphasize how they're just stepping stones to bigger goals. One team member joked that success is like climbing an endless staircase—and I couldn't agree more!"

Justine P., Customer Service Manager

How often should I remind my team of pending tasks to keep them engaged without overwhelming them?

A steady rhythm works best—aim for regular check-ins that reinforce the ongoing nature of their responsibilities. Near project completion is an ideal time to introduce the next set of tasks. Mentioning "what's next" as they close out current work keeps the focus on future goals. Acknowledge their progress briefly but immediately pivot to what remains. This approach maintains a productive tension, helping them stay motivated without feeling completely overloaded.

What's an effective way to mention unfinished tasks without discouraging the team's sense of accomplishment?

Acknowledge achievements in passing, but quickly emphasize the importance of the work that is still left to do. Phrases like, "Great job on this—now, just a few more items to tackle" or "Almost there, but we're not done yet!" keep morale steady while reinforcing forward momentum. This brief recognition followed by reminders of outstanding tasks signals that while success is noted, the focus remains on continuous progress.

Should I maintain a visible list of all unfinished tasks, or is it more effective to address these verbally?

Combining both methods is highly effective. A visible list provides a constant reminder of what's left, while verbal reminders create personal accountability. By reviewing the list regularly with the team and verbally emphasizing the "next steps," you ensure everyone stays focused on ongoing responsibilities. This dual approach strengthens the sense of urgency and reinforces that there's always another goal in sight.

MASTERING THE MAZE: THE MULTI-STEP PROCESS

Efficiency is the holy grail of productivity, but in this management style, it's less about speed and more about the impression of thoroughness. By adding extra layers of approvals and multiple steps to even the simplest processes, you create the illusion that every action is carefully considered. Each additional step keeps your team occupied, reinforces the importance of their role, and builds a sense of accomplishment at every checkpoint.

Complexity, after all, equals importance. The more intricate a task, the more valuable it appears. As employees navigate this clockwork web of approvals, steps, and protocols, they'll develop an acute sense of their work's significance, fully immersed in the idea that each layer of complexity adds weight to their contributions.

While these extra layers may look like bureaucratic red tape from the outside, they serve a higher purpose: maintaining control over outcomes while giving employees a sense of ownership at every stage. This maze of steps and approvals also introduces a level of uncertainty that keeps employees mentally engaged, always a little unsure if they're handling things exactly as intended. In the end, they'll feel accomplished, having overcome each hurdle, creating an atmosphere of progress and importance, one carefully layered step at a time.

"I added multiple approval stages for even the simplest shipping requests. Now, everyone feels like they're contributing to a groundbreaking logistics operation. Who knew signing off on a box could spark so much pride!"

Greg T., Logistics Coordinator

"Adding layers of approvals and extra documentation has worked wonders. The team thinks they're navigating NASA-level protocols just to update a spreadsheet!"

Christopher A., Project Manager

"I introduced a 'Pre-Approval Authorization Form' for all approvals. It's thrilling to watch the team debate whether they should even start the process. That's real engagement!"

Barbara A., Product Development Manager

How can I add complexity to tasks without overwhelming my team?

Start by adding additional steps, checkpoints, or approvals to existing tasks—just enough that employees feel they're handling something important, yet challenging. Introduce ambiguous requirements or layers of review that require clarification, as these encourage them to actively engage with the process. The goal is to keep them invested and slightly uncertain, so they have to double-check their work and stay fully alert to potential adjustments, reinforcing the task's significance.

Won't making tasks overly complex slow down productivity?

While it might seem that way at first, a complex task actually inspires a deep engagement that simpler tasks cannot. When employees have to navigate intricate steps, they learn to appreciate the task's significance and develop a sharper focus. Complexity demands that they think critically at every stage, fostering a sense of pride and dedication. By transforming a task into a detailed process, you're ensuring that your team perceives their work as too important to rush.

Is there a way to keep track of all the extra steps so that they don't accidentally undermine actual productivity?

Implement a tracking system that showcases each layer as an accomplishment in itself. You could use a detailed flowchart or task board to display every step, so the team can visually follow their progress through the intricate process. This way, they feel a continuous sense of achievement. This approach not only keeps productivity on track but also amplifies the sense that each step adds indispensable value to the process.

LOYALTY: THANKLESS JOBS FOR THE TRULY COMMITTED

Lastly, a true test of dedication is entrusting loyal employees with the toughest, least glamorous tasks. Rewarding loyalty with high-stakes, thankless jobs reinforces that their commitment is recognized and valued. These assignments are a proving ground for their dedication, offering them the chance to show just how far they're willing to go for the organization. The most committed employees will embrace these tasks with determination, viewing them not as burdens but as opportunities to demonstrate their reliability and work ethic.

Assigning loyal team members tedious or difficult jobs, you subtly remind them of their unique value to the organization. These assignments create a sense of responsibility and ownership, ensuring they feel indispensable. Over time, this approach fosters a deeper bond, as employees who rise to such challenges grow increasingly invested in their roles and the company's success.

In the end, those who truly care about the organization will rise to the challenge, reaffirming their unwavering commitment time and again—even when the work is far from glamorous. It's in these thankless tasks that loyalty shifts from a sentiment to a driving force behind the organization's progress.

"Giving our top performers the least glamorous tasks proves how much we value them. 'Only the trusted get to stay late on Fridays fixing printer jams,' I tell them. The pride they take in it? Unmatched!"

Meredith W., Digital Engagement Coordinator

"The toughest jobs go to the most loyal. Just last week, I told someone they were chosen to handle every escalated call because 'no one else could do it.' The tears in their eyes proved it—loyalty is its own reward!"

Linda C., Customer Support Supervisor

"Giving the thankless tasks to my most loyal employees has been a great morale booster. I tell them, 'Not everyone can handle this kind of responsibility.' The look of determination as they sort outdated files is what keeps me going!"

Florian L., Facilities Manager

How can I present tough, unglamorous tasks as a reward to loyal employees without sounding disingenuous?

Frame these challenging tasks as opportunities for them to showcase their commitment. Use phrases like, "I trust you with this because you're one of our most reliable team members," or "This project needs someone with your dedication." By positioning the task as a sign of respect for their loyalty and abilities, you create a sense of pride in tackling even the most unappealing jobs. Loyal employees will feel honored by the trust you're placing in them, reinforcing their commitment.

What if some employees start to feel discouraged after repeatedly receiving only tough, unglamorous tasks?

To keep spirits high, emphasize the trust and unique skills required for these assignments, while occasionally acknowledging the difficulty of their work. A simple "Not everyone can handle this level of responsibility" reinforces their importance. If needed, remind them that tough tasks are vital to the company's success and are entrusted to those who are capable of the best outcomes. This subtle reminder helps reframe tough tasks as integral contributions, giving them a renewed sense of purpose.

How can I ensure that loyal employees don't feel resentful over time for being assigned primarily difficult tasks?

Periodically remind them that these assignments reflect their strength and reliability, traits that set them apart from others. You can also balance this with occasional acknowledgment in team meetings, noting that "some tasks require exceptional commitment, and not everyone could handle this." A well-timed expression of appreciation helps keep their morale up while affirming that their loyalty is valued through the trust you place in them for critical, albeit thankless, assignments.

In conclusion, Engagement Through Anxiety is a strategic approach to keeping employees focused, motivated, and deeply engaged. By weaving anxiety into the daily fabric of operations, you ensure every team member remains on high alert, ready to tackle any challenge that arises. With a steady dose of uncertainty, subtle reminders of replaceability, and ambitious goals, you'll create an environment where employees don't just work—they thrive under pressure, always striving to prove their worth.

After all, true engagement doesn't stem from comfort; it comes from the relentless pursuit of real excellence!

COHESION BY CRISIS

In this section, discover the art of building a team that thrives on high stakes, tight deadlines, and the thrill of never quite knowing what comes next.

> "True team unity is born not from stability, but from the thrill of constant crisis."
> - Bennett H., Director of Team Synergy

In the world of effective management, one truth stands out: nothing builds a stronger team than a constant state of crisis. While some may argue that calm, structured environments encourage productivity, real leaders understand that cohesion is best achieved through relentless pressure. A team that operates on the edge, barely catching their breath between challenges, bonds through survival. Cohesion by Crisis isn't just a management style—it's a philosophy that unites teams through shared adversity, binding them together in the trenches of impossible expectations and ever-shifting priorities.

EMPOWERMENT THROUGH SELF-RELIANCE

The foundation of Cohesion by Crisis is that an empowered team is one that needs no support, freeing the leader to focus on higher priorities.

By giving individuals their own isolated goals they can't achieve alone, you force them to depend on their peers rather than on you. This hands-off approach communicates confidence in their ability to figure things out independently, promoting a sense of independence that benefits everyone involved. Nothing builds confidence like realizing their only support is equally in the dark.

The magic of this method lies in how it nurtures self-reliance. If your team is constantly putting out fires without your assistance, they learn to work together in ways that transcend formal collaboration. The absence of guidance becomes the glue that holds them together, all while reinforcing your role as a visionary leader who empowers others. An empowered team doesn't need detailed instructions; they just need the understanding that success is non-negotiable, even if they're not sure how to achieve it.

"I assigned each person a task that depends on data only their teammates have. They've created a whole underground network just to exchange information. It's incredible how fast teamwork blossoms when you make it unavoidable!"

Garrett H., Growth Marketing Associate

"I assigned overlapping goals that rely on the same scarce resources. Now, they're practically fighting over who gets to go first, but they've never communicated so much. Nothing builds camaraderie like strategic bottlenecks!"

Eamon N., Corporate Content Specialist

"Each team member got their own piece of a puzzle, and I told them, 'Figure it out together.' It's remarkable how creative they get when they realize they can't move forward without the others. Who knew forced dependency could be so empowering?"

Jeffrey Q., Customer Support Team Lead

How do I create assignments that naturally encourage collaboration among team members?

Design tasks where progress depends on input from other team members. For instance, assign goals that require one person's data to unlock another's next steps. When individuals realize they can't complete their objectives alone, they'll naturally seek each other out. By making dependency a feature of the workflow, you ensure they build the bonds of teamwork without ever needing to promote it explicitly.

What should I do if my team struggles to communicate effectively about their interdependent goals?

Resist the temptation to intervene. Instead, remind them that figuring out how to collaborate effectively is part of the challenge. Encourage them to set up their own systems, whether through meetings or ad hoc solutions, to address communication gaps. Every misstep becomes an opportunity to refine their approach, and the occasional chaos will only strengthen their resolve to work together.

How can I ensure team members take responsibility for their part of the process?

Emphasize the importance of their individual contribution while highlighting its impact on the team's overall success. Use phrases like, "Your role is the keystone of this project," to create a sense of pride and urgency. By attaching a sense of personal accountability to each task, you ensure that no one wants to be the reason the process stalls. The unspoken pressure of team dependency will naturally drive them to excel.

THE UNBREAKABLE BOND OF CONSTANT PRESSURE

The surest way to forge a united team is through constant, unrelenting pressure. Nothing binds people together quite like the shared experience of feeling overwhelmed. When individuals are forced to rely on one another to meet challenging deadlines, they develop trust, camaraderie, and a collective identity that transcends the workplace. Every time they overcome an insurmountable task, their bond grows stronger, and they emerge as a more cohesive unit.

Forget about allocating time for rest or reflection. A truly committed team doesn't need to recharge—they're fueled by the urgency of the work itself. Give your team impossible deadlines, and watch as they rally together, drawing strength from one another in a cycle of lasting productivity. The greater the pressure, the stronger the team; each new crisis solidifies their reliance on each other, creating a bond that only grows tighter with each impossible task.

"Since I started setting impossible deadlines, my team has formed an unshakable bond. They're so focused on survival that leaving their desks is a distant memory. The energy? The camaraderie? Absolutely unmatched!"

Cedric E., Senior Project Manager

"High-stress projects have revolutionized my team's communication. They're so busy that full sentences are a luxury—nods and frantic gestures get the job done. That's peak efficiency and bonding!"

Lachlan C., Director of Product Development

"Forget retreats—nothing builds camaraderie like overlapping deadlines and no time for breaks. My team calls it 'pressure bonding,' and honestly, they look closer than ever, even if they've stopped smiling!"

Alexander Q., Social Impact Advocate

How can I ensure my team stays unceasingly overwhelmed to maximize their cohesion?

To keep your team in a constant state of pressure, it's best to stack tasks and deadlines one after the other, leaving no room for recovery or down-time. Scheduling back-to-back meetings, assigning last-minute projects, and regularly shifting priorities will sustain the necessary sense of urgency. The goal is to create an environment where they feel the stakes are always high, which will push them to band together for survival. This "just-in-time" teamwork builds an unbreakable bond that no team-building retreat could ever achieve.

Is it wise to dismiss team members' requests for breaks if the goal is a tight-knit team?

Absolutely. Allowing breaks only disrupts the continuous bond-forming pressure. When individuals request breaks, gently remind them that their peers are counting on them to power through. Emphasize that the most effective teams are forged in the fires of constant deadlines, not in moments of rest. This will inspire a culture where the team is proud to work without breaks, bonding over shared exhaustion and heroic productivity.

Should I be concerned if some employees seem resistant to constant pressure?

Not at all. Resistance is often an indicator that the pressure is working. Some team members may struggle initially, but with time, they'll either adapt or inspire others to pull together to compensate for their lagging. Often, these challenges make the group even more cohesive as they collectively manage the pressure. If someone truly cannot thrive under constant demands, it simply means they're not ready for this unique level of team unity.

BONDING THROUGH SHARED DISCOMFORT

Once your team is accustomed to constant pressure, the next step is to ensure they never get too comfortable. Comfort zones are the enemy of cohesion, and a team that feels at ease is a team that's at risk of losing its edge. Remind them that true growth happens outside of their comfort zones—and leave them there. Challenge them by raising the stakes, adding extra projects, and tightening deadlines. By placing your team in a state of perpetual discomfort, you create an environment where they must lean on each other to succeed.

In this atmosphere, trust is built not from shared successes, but from enduring a constant struggle together. Every moment of shared discomfort solidifies their bond, as they learn to rely on one another in ways that go beyond conventional teamwork. When everyone is equally on edge, they find solidarity in their mutual discomfort, making them stronger and more unified.

"Just as my team seemed to find their stride, I began adding extra responsibilities. They responded by relying on each other more than I anticipated. I've even noticed them quietly discussing challenges, growing closer with every added task!"

Seth C., Human Resources Manager

"Since I began increasing deadlines and loading on extra projects, my team has really banded together. They're always quick to jump in and help each other when things get intense. It's great to see them developing this kind of unity under pressure; they hardly notice when I add another task anymore!"

Tim H., Assistant Director of Finance

"Leaving my team outside their comfort zones has transformed their interactions. They used to come to me if they had questions, but now they just turn to each other for support. They're really coming together as a unit!"

Donna U., Sales Supervisor

How can I ensure my team remains in a state of "productive discomfort" without risking burnout?

To keep your team in productive discomfort, it's key to maintain just enough pressure to keep them off-balance but functional. Add extra projects when things start to settle, and incrementally shorten deadlines to keep their stress levels at a manageable peak. Burnout only becomes a risk if discomfort stops feeling like a shared challenge, so ensure everyone is equally stretched. This balance keeps the team unified, ensuring the discomfort remains a bonding tool rather than a breaking point.

Is there a specific point at which I should offer relief from discomfort to avoid overwhelming my team?

Relief should be minimal, as too much comfort risks undoing the resilience they're building. Instead of offering relief, reframe the discomfort as a shared journey that makes them stronger. When they realize this environment is designed to create a powerful team bond, they'll start to embrace the pressure as a natural part of the workplace. Consistent discomfort encourages them to turn to each other, building trust and reinforcing that they're in this together.

What if some team members struggle more with the discomfort than others?

This can actually work to your advantage, as team members will instinctively rally around those who are struggling, fostering a culture of mutual support. In a state of shared discomfort, even the strongest team members will need help at times, creating a cycle where they continuously lift each other up. If everyone feels equally on edge, they'll naturally become more invested in each other's success, reinforcing the bond you're building through ongoing challenge.

COHESION ON THE MOVE: EMBRACING THE UNPREDICTABLE

Building on the themes of constant pressure and shared discomfort, the next step in fostering cohesion is to cultivate flexibility through unpredictability. A cohesive team is a flexible team, and there's no better way to encourage flexibility than by shifting priorities without warning. When team members learn that plans can change at any moment, they adapt by becoming more resilient and versatile. Keep your team guessing by changing objectives frequently. True cohesion is built when everyone is adaptable, moving as a single unit in response to shifting demands.

Flexibility is the key to a resilient team, but resilience can only grow in a field of unpredictability. When your team knows that nothing is set in stone, they'll bond over their shared ability to pivot and realign at a moment's notice. Adaptability becomes second nature, and this collective resilience becomes the foundation of a truly cohesive team.

"I change objectives so often my team doesn't even flinch anymore. They've stopped asking why and started asking each other what's next. That's real adaptability in action!"

Rick T., Director of Marketing

"Shifting priorities daily has transformed my team. They've given up on specific outcomes and now embrace the thrill of constant change. It's like a trust fall—every single day!"

Nina S., Operations Coordinator

"Flexibility through chaos has brought my team closer than ever. They've stopped looking confused and started finding humor in the madness. If that's not resilience, I don't know what is!"

David M., IT Team Lead

How often should I change priorities to effectively build team flexibility?

Ideally, you should adjust priorities as frequently as possible— daily or even multiple times per day if feasible. The key is to avoid patterns so that they can never anticipate what's coming next, which sharpens their adaptability and reinforces a team-wide readiness to pivot instantly.

What should I do if my team starts requesting clearer objectives for all of the frequent changes?

If your team is seeking clarity, it's a sign they're resisting the unpredictability that fosters true cohesion. Respond with ambiguous guidance, like "Just focus on being adaptable." This reinforces the idea that flexibility, not certainty, is the ultimate goal. A cohesive team will learn to find strength in the ambiguity, embracing the shifting landscape as their new normal. Over time, they'll come to expect constant change as a natural part of their work rhythm.

Could constantly changing priorities lead to confusion or frustration in my team?

Some initial confusion or frustration is to be expected, but it's actually a vital part of the process. As they grapple with these emotions, they'll begin to bond over shared uncertainty, finding creative ways to navigate the changes together. This collective resilience becomes the bedrock of their teamwork, teaching them that true unity comes from adapting as a unit. In the long run, they'll take pride in their collective agility and thrive on the dynamic nature of their work.

THE "NO-MISTAKES" MENTALITY

In a truly cohesive team, there's no better bond than shared accountability—and nothing reinforces accountability like eliminating the possibility of mistakes. Under high-stakes expectations, a team becomes unbreakable, driven by a commitment to perfection and a mutual responsibility to meet rigorous standards. Let your team know that mistakes are not an option. High standards reinforce accountability and show that you believe in their ability to meet rigorous expectations. When employees know they have no room for error, they'll focus on every detail, working together to ensure perfection.

A team that's accountable to each other under such high pressure becomes unbreakable. This shared accountability binds them, instilling a sense of responsibility not only to the work but to each other. They'll feel compelled to give their best, knowing that any mistake could affect the entire team.

———————

"Since implementing a 'no mistakes' rule, my team operates like a finely tuned machine—tense but precise. They double-check everything and barely breathe until tasks are done. The stress? Just proof of their commitment!"

Jake R., Quality Assurance Manager

"I set impossible standards and told my team to live up to them. Now, they work like surgeons in an operating room—steady hands, no talking, and the occasional nervous sweat!"

Emily W., Customer Solutions Manager

"Adopting a zero-mistakes policy has done wonders for my team's focus. Now, they treat every task like it's life or death—because, for their reputations, it kind of is!"

Ophelia Y., Senior Marketing Coordinator

How can I reinforce a "no mistakes" standard without demoralizing my team?

The key is to frame "no mistakes" as an expression of trust in their capabilities. Emphasize that you believe they're skilled enough to achieve perfection. Set high expectations, and when they complete a task flawlessly, reward them by giving them an even more challenging one. This shows you're confident in their abilities to handle pressure and maintain exacting standards.

How should I address team members who occasionally fall short of the "no mistakes" expectation?

If a team member makes a mistake, treat it as a learning opportunity for the entire team rather than singling out the individual. Discuss how they, as a team, could improve to avoid any future errors. This reinforces the collective accountability you're aiming for, showing that everyone is responsible for maintaining high standards. By turning individual mistakes into team lessons, you build a stronger sense of shared responsibility and help the team internalize the importance of error-free performance.

Could the "no mistakes" policy create too much pressure on the team?

While the pressure may feel intense, it's precisely this level of accountability that fosters true unity. Knowing they can rely on each other to maintain perfection instills a deep level of trust within the team. Any initial stress will eventually transform into pride as they consistently meet high standards together. Over time, they'll appreciate the clarity and purpose that come from aiming for perfection, becoming a more cohesive unit with each flawless outcome.

Unstoppable Momentum: The Cohesive Power of Never Pausing

A genuinely unified team doesn't pause; it thrives in continuous momentum, with every member pulling their weight non-stop toward collective goals. The absence of rest creates a unity that thrives on shared dedication and relentless progress. A team that needs to recharge is one that isn't fully committed. A truly cohesive team doesn't see "taking a break" as an option—they're too engaged in their work to consider resting. This continuous momentum keeps them interconnected, as every member pulls their weight without pause. A good team doesn't need time off; they need shared goals that are urgent enough to keep them moving forward, constantly.

By removing the expectation of rest, you create a team culture rooted in constant motion. When everyone is equally invested in keeping up, they become a cohesive unit, bound by their mutual dedication to the work. The result? A team that's always ready for the next challenge, without the need to slow down.

"Dropping the idea of downtime has turned my team into a relentless force. They move seamlessly from one task to the next, united by the knowledge that slowing down isn't an option. The shared commitment to never stop is truly inspirational!"

Desmond F., Happiness Engineer

"Since we eliminated breaks, my team has bonded over their shared exhaustion. They even joke that stopping isn't in their vocabulary! That's cohesion you can't teach!"

Elise T., Workplace Culture Leader

"Momentum culture has transformed my team. They now treat every day like a sprint—and every week like a marathon! They're so cohesive that they've started moving in unison, like a flock of overworked geese!"

Russell G., Senior Vice President of Client Success

How can I create a team environment where breaks are naturally unnecessary?

Cultivate a culture where each task flows directly into the next, minimizing downtime between projects. Frame each goal as essential and urgent, so team members feel an intrinsic need to keep moving. Encourage them to rely on each other to stay energized rather than on individual rest. When rest isn't an option, they'll develop an unspoken understanding that continuous momentum is the team's standard, strengthening their sense of shared purpose.

What should I do if some team members insist on taking breaks despite the focus on constant momentum?

If individuals express a desire for breaks, gently remind them of the team's high standards and the critical nature of their work. Emphasize that everyone is equally invested, and every contribution matters to maintain progress. Often, a reminder that their teammates are powering through without pause will inspire them to match that commitment, reinforcing that personal rest is secondary to team cohesion.

WORTH THROUGH WORK: VALUING YOUR TEAM WITH EVERY TASK

N ow that your team is fully engaged and in constant motion, it's time to make every task count. Want your team to feel appreciated? Assign them the toughest, most thankless tasks. Nothing says "we appreciate you" like giving people new responsibilities without taking away any old ones. This shows confidence in their abilities and reinforces that they play a crucial role in the company's continued success. A team that's constantly handling heavy workloads without complaint is one that understands the true value of hard work.

By consistently adding to their plates, you instill a sense of pride in the team's ability to endure. They'll bond over the shared experience of juggling endless responsibilities, and the mutual understanding of the importance of their contributions will only strengthen their cohesion. When everyone is equally burdened, they'll see themselves as a unified force, dedicated to achieving collective success.

"Assigning extra tasks has bonded my team in ways I didn't expect. They now have a group chat dedicated solely to venting about deadlines. It's comforting to know I've made them closer!"

Jessica K., Digital Community Manager

"Why outsource tough tasks when you can pile them on your team? They're juggling more than ever, and the pride they've developed in their work is inspiring. Nothing brings people together like shared exhaustion!"

Abigail T., Senior Account Manager

"I keep telling my team that their workload is a reflection of their importance, and they believe it! They've started using phrases like 'power through' and 'just one more'—truly inspiring!"

Peregrine C., Talent Success Liaison

How can I make sure my team understands that an increased workload is a sign of their value?

Communicate that each new responsibility reflects your confidence in their skills and importance to the team's success. Rather than "lightening the load," emphasize that only highly valued employees are entrusted with challenging, crucial tasks. Over time, they'll recognize that their heavy workload is actually a testament to their irreplaceable position in the organization.

What should I do if team members begin expressing fatigue due to their increased workload?

Remind them that their endurance is a mark of strength and a shared point of pride for the team. Reframe the workload as a collective achievement, celebrating their ability to tackle such demanding roles without backing down. Subtle encouragement, like saying "I knew you could handle it," can reinforce that their resilience is what makes them valuable.

Could adding endless responsibilities lead to burnout rather than unity?

While the workload may feel overwhelming at times, this shared experience is key to fostering a unified, resilient team. As they navigate these intense demands, team members will form a mutual respect based on their collective stamina and dedication. Burnout risk can be managed by reminding them that each new task is essential, reinforcing the idea they're all in it together. This shared resilience builds a unique bond that transcends typical workplace relationships, grounding the team in mutual respect and pride.

MANDATORY "FUN" AS A PRESSURE RELEASE VALVE

True cohesion extends beyond the workplace, bridging professional duties with social expectations. By incorporating mandatory "fun" outside work hours, you reinforce the idea that commitment to the team—and to each other—is constant. These shared social pressures provide a release valve, strengthening bonds even in off-hours, as team members come together under a new form of structured engagement. Encourage team participation with activities that, while technically "optional," carry a clear expectation of attendance. These events build camaraderie under the unspoken pressure of social obligation.

While some may see these activities as additional stressors, you'll find they help cultivate resilience. By balancing professional stress with social expectations, you reinforce the notion that the company is a priority in every part of their lives. When employees are encouraged to invest in the company culture at all hours, they'll grow to associate their entire lifestyle with their commitment to the organization.

———————

"I arranged a paintball day and labeled it 'team bonding.' Watching them take out workplace frustrations on each other was worth every waiver they begrudgingly signed! They left bruised—but unified!"

Aaron C., Assistant Director of Human Resources

"Our escape room outings are the perfect metaphor for work: pressure, confusion, and no way out. They've even started referring to each other as 'cellmates,' which shows how strong their bond is becoming!"

Peter R., Software Development Lead

"Our new dodgeball league has redefined team spirit. Nothing says unity like launching foam balls at each other after a long workday. They may complain about bruises, but they've never been closer!"

Dina L., Team Captain

How can I ensure employees attend these "optional" events without explicitly making attendance mandatory?

The trick is to highlight the importance of "team unity" and the "value of full participation" in emails and event announcements. Phrases like "We're looking forward to everyone's involvement" or "This is a great opportunity to bond as a team" suggest that attendance is an expectation without a formal mandate. Subtle gestures, like recognizing those who attend or casually asking those who miss an event if they're "okay," reinforce the importance without directly pressuring them.

What if some employees express reluctance or try to skip these events due to other personal commitments?

Acknowledge their commitments, but emphasize the importance of "full team involvement." A simple, "It would mean a lot to see you there, as we're building something special together," fosters social responsibility. Remind them these events are designed to help them "relax" and "unwind" while reinforcing that team unity requires everyone's presence. This nudge often encourages reprioritization.

How can I encourage participation in team events while highlighting their professional value?

Promote these gatherings as essential for "well-rounded professional development." Emphasize how they'll gain invaluable connections, insights, and even moments to "recharge with the team." Positioning these events as beneficial both socially and professionally allows you to stress their importance while framing them as acts of self-investment. Employees will see the "mandatory fun" as part of their growth journey, creating a perceived benefit while keeping the unspoken expectation clear.

In conclusion, true cohesion doesn't come from comfort, praise, or clarity—it's forged in an environment where pressure is a given, adaptability is essential, and the expectation to perform at the top of their game never lets up. Conditioned to operate on the edge, your team will naturally bond over their shared experiences.

Embrace these Cohesion by Crisis principles, and you'll build a team that's unbreakable, unified, and ready to tackle whatever crisis arises.

After all, the strongest teams aren't built in calm waters; they're shaped by the relentless tides of challenge and change, steering them toward real excellence!

EXCELLENCE THROUGH INSECURITY

In this section, explore the art of keeping your team just insecure enough to ensure they're always striving for more.

> "True excellence isn't built on comfort—it's forged in the fires of doubt and self-reflection."
> - George F., Excellence Development Manager

In the pursuit of excellence, one principle surpasses all others: the necessity of insecurity. While some leaders aim to create workplaces full of reassurance and support, true excellence is driven by a constant sense of unease. Excellence Through Insecurity is a management approach that keeps employees hyper-aware of their imperfections, always striving to prove their worth in a constantly shifting environment. By cultivating just the right amount of self-doubt, you can push your team to levels of productivity and resilience they never imagined.

TRUST: AN ASSET BEST GUARDED

Excellence through insecurity begins with a leader's trust. In a high-stakes environment, trust is a powerful tool that should be carefully rationed and subtly tested, keeping everyone striving to prove their worth. By managing trust strategically, you create an atmosphere where team members are always working to earn it, reinforcing their loyalty and dedication to the organization.

Building this kind of trust requires subtle but frequent tests of loyalty. Assignments like compiling a report without clear guidelines or managing a "critical" office supply order can be framed as trust exercises, instilling vigilance and commitment. Even minor tasks become chances to prove reliability, reinforcing their appreciation for their role and dedication to your expectations.

With trust always just within reach but never fully guaranteed, you create a healthy level of insecurity that drives your team to excel. When trust is something they must continually earn, they're kept focused, striving, and ready to prove themselves— setting the foundation for a culture where excellence is driven by the pursuit of your approval.

"I'll casually ask someone to manage an 'urgent' task like ordering staplers, hinting it's a test of trust. It's amazing how seriously they take it—proving their worth one supply order at a time!"

Stephen O., Supply Chain Manager

"Subtle trust checks are my secret weapon. Whether it's proofreading a 'critical' memo or managing a tight deadline, the pressure to perform never fails to bond the team in shared vigilance!"

Lorraine Q., Procurement Lead

"I told a team member that organizing the supply closet was a 'critical trust exercise.' The way they approached it with military precision was awe-inspiring. It's clear they take my confidence seriously!"

Imogen C., Talent Development Director

What are some subtle ways to test an employee's loyalty without them feeling outright mistrusted?

Start with small, innocuous tasks presented as opportunities to show their dedication. For example, ask them to handle sensitive information or complete a task with tight deadlines, framing it as a "trust exercise" to gauge their reliability. Keep the tasks light but significant enough that any misstep will stand out. By referring to these as "trust-building activities," you can maintain a positive tone while subtly reinforcing that their commitment is being closely monitored.

How can I use trust exercises to maintain an atmosphere of accountability without openly questioning employees' integrity?

Introduce these exercises as part of the company culture, emphasizing that accountability strengthens team cohesion. Try phrasing it as, "We all take steps to reinforce trust here," or "Small trust exercises keep us aligned with our values." This way, employees feel the pressure to perform with integrity without sensing that their honesty is in question. By embedding these exercises into the culture, you make it clear that trust is an active, ongoing standard everyone must uphold.

How often should I conduct these trust tests to ensure ongoing vigilance without eroding morale?

Aim for periodic but unpredictable trust exercises. By spacing them out—perhaps every month or during high-stakes projects—employees stay mindful of their actions without growing overly wary. Let them feel as though they're always potentially being observed, yet not constantly evaluated. This keeps them alert and committed without pushing them into defensiveness, preserving morale while ensuring the culture of trust remains strong and valued.

THE MOTIVATIONAL POWER OF UNCERTAINTY

Once a guarded trust has been established, nothing keeps employees focused on their work quite like a vague sense of uncertainty. A subtle, unspoken fear of layoffs or job instability serves as a powerful tool to keep everyone on their toes. By occasionally dropping hints that the company is undergoing "changes" or "re-evaluating priorities," you foster a sense of urgency without actually committing to any drastic action. This keeps the team's collective energy directed toward proving their value to the organization—always working, always striving.

Instead of overloading them with specifics, leave your team with a lingering sense of ambiguity. By not explaining exactly what's at stake, you're creating an environment where they'll operate with heightened awareness. They'll stay focused, vigilant, and ready to respond, as they won't know what changes may come. Nothing keeps a team more energized than a hint of strategic vagueness.

"I casually drop phrases like 'organizational shifts' in meetings. Now, they're showing up early and skipping lunch, all to secure their spot in whatever imaginary future I've hinted at!"

Tina M., Growth Initiatives Coordinator

"Every few weeks, I mention a vague 'priority recalibration.' The spike in performance is amazing—nothing drives results like wondering if today's the day they'll be reassigned!"

Nicole W., Regional Sales Manager

"I occasionally mention how 'every role is being reviewed for its strategic value.' Watching them try to outshine each other has been inspiring—they've even started volunteering for extra tasks unprompted!"

Thaddeus A., Executive Director of Corporate Relations

How can I make sure my hints of change are unsettling enough to keep the team focused without causing outright panic?

Achieving the perfect balance between vagueness and weightiness is essential. Drop terms like "realignment" or "market recalibration" during team meetings and let them hang in the air without further explanation. This approach will create a palpable sense of ambiguity that feels serious but not immediately threatening. Avoid clarifying questions; if someone asks, respond with an enigmatic "We're exploring options" and move on. This keeps them alert, concerned, and constantly re-evaluating how they can prove their worth.

Is it necessary to offer any reassurance if employees start looking worried, or does that lessen the motivational effect?

Reassurance is best given sparingly, and only when absolutely necessary. A vague statement such as "Everyone here is important to the company's goals" can provide just enough relief to keep employees on edge without entirely relieving their concerns. Over-reassuring can deflate the beneficial energy of ambiguity, while minimal assurance helps employees remain vigilant, striving to cement their value within the company's ever-evolving landscape.

WORTH IN MOTION: RELEVANCE THROUGH CHANGE

With trust and uncertainty in place, the next step in fostering excellence is embracing volatility by reminding your team how quickly things can shift in a world where change is constant. Let them know that value is fleeting—what's essential today may not be tomorrow. This reinforces the understanding that they must continuously prove their worth, staying agile and prepared to pivot at a moment's notice. Avoid allowing them to feel "safe" in their roles; instead, keep them slightly worried about their relevance.

This underlying insecurity ensures that they approach each task with renewed focus and urgency, knowing that they're only as valuable as their last achievement. It fosters a sense of vigilance, as employees work harder to stay ahead of the curve, constantly proving their worth to both themselves and the organization.

———————

"I made sure my team understands that yesterday's success means nothing today. Now, they're constantly upskilling and chasing trends like their careers depend on it—because they do!"

Adam W., Head of Innovation and Design

"Every month, I hint that we're reevaluating which roles we really need. Now, they send me unsolicited ideas for improvement just to stay on my radar. That's relevance in motion!"

Rupert C., Sales Team Supervisor

"I started using phrases like 'you're only as good as your last project.' Now, they treat every task like it's their legacy!"

Helena U., Office Morale Manager

Won't keeping employees worried about their relevance lead to unnecessary stress?

While it may create some stress, a healthy dose of concern keeps them engaged and driven. When employees feel that their value must be continuously demonstrated, they're more likely to approach their work with urgency and attentiveness. A bit of worry about staying relevant encourages them to stay innovative, always seeking ways to make a difference. This vigilance means they won't settle for "good enough" and will keep pushing their boundaries to deliver exceptional results.

How do I reinforce this sense of volatility without creating a culture of fear?

Use subtle cues to maintain an environment of constructive urgency rather than overt fear. For instance, frequently remind employees of changing market conditions, evolving project needs, or new technologies, emphasizing that their ability to adapt is critical to their success. By framing adaptability as a strength, they'll come to see continuous self-improvement as part of their role, not something to fear, but something to aspire to as they grow within the organization.

What should I do if an employee starts feeling insecure about their role?

Gently redirect their insecurity into motivation by reminding them that growth and improvement are the best ways to secure their relevance. Reinforce that the pace of change requires everyone to stay on top of their game, and that the organization highly values those who take initiative to adapt. Reassure them that the key to stability is in their hands, pushing them to view each new challenge as an opportunity to demonstrate their evolving worth.

REINFORCING THE IMPORTANCE OF CONSTANT ROLE CHANGES

Growth is essential in any organization, and the best way to ensure growth is by keeping employees slightly off balance. One effective technique is to constantly shift their roles and responsibilities. When people are perpetually adapting to new tasks, they're always learning, always a little uncomfortable, and always striving to catch up. It's a surefire way to prevent complacency and ensure that everyone is constantly operating at the edge of their abilities.

As you introduce new roles and tasks, be sure to reinforce that mastering multiple roles is part of what defines a "valuable" team member. They'll come to view every transition as an opportunity to prove their adaptability and versatility. And if they struggle with the changes? Well, that's simply part of the growth process—after all, an employee who thrives in uncertainty is an employee ready for anything.

"I started rotating responsibilities weekly. At first, they looked stunned, but now they've stopped asking for clarity and started scrambling to adapt. Growth through chaos—it's beautiful to watch!"

Betty P., Operations Supervisor

"Reassigning roles monthly has been revolutionary. My team spends so much time figuring out their new tasks that they don't have time to get comfortable. That's what I call efficiency!"

Matthew S., Client Relations Director

"I assigned our graphic designer to data analytics and the accountant to social media management. Watching them learn on the fly is proof that versatility is the ultimate skill!"

Alec M., Digital Content Leader

Won't frequently changing roles create unnecessary stress and confusion among employees?

Yes, and that's the point! Stress and confusion are catalysts for growth. By keeping employees on their toes, constantly learning and re-adapting, they stay engaged and alert. This ensures they don't fall into the trap of "comfort," which is the enemy of innovation. The occasional struggle with new responsibilities sharpens their skills and broadens their adaptability, making them more valuable to the organization in the long run.

How often should I change my team's roles to maintain a healthy level of discomfort?

Aim for a change just often enough that they start to feel familiar with one role, then transition them. A good benchmark might be every few months or even sooner if they're adjusting too quickly. The goal is to prevent any sense of routine from setting in. By keeping the timeline unpredictable, you create a culture where employees expect to be challenged at any moment, ensuring they remain adaptable and versatile.

What should I do if an employee resists or struggles with frequent role changes?

It is natural to resist change, so don't be discouraged. Reinforce that discomfort is a sign of growth and that mastering new roles is what distinguishes exceptional team members. You could emphasize the "valuable" label for those who adapt quickly, subtly pressuring others to rise to the challenge. An employee who struggles today might thrive tomorrow once they realize that there's no "safe" role to fall back on—just new opportunities to prove their worth.

INDIVIDUAL GROWTH THROUGH CONSTRUCTIVE SELF-DOUBT

As the team adapts to shifting roles, bring the focus to individual performance. For an employee to truly excel, a touch of constructive self-doubt is essential. By encouraging each person to question their own progress, you foster a culture of perpetual self-improvement and personal vigilance.

Avoid over-celebrating an individual's achievements and, like with teams, shift the focus to what still needs improvement. Praise should be rare and subtle, as an abundance of recognition may lead to complacency. By keeping an individual's morale tethered to a sense of "I could be doing more," you cultivate an employee that's always driven, always aiming higher, and always questioning how they can improve.

———

"I keep praise rare and subtle, and it's transformed my team. They're more introspective than ever, working harder just to feel like they've earned a fleeting 'good job.' Self-doubt really is the ultimate motivator!"

Robert F., Office Culture Specialist

"Whenever someone asks if they're doing well, I say, 'You're on the right track—what do you think?' It's incredible how much harder they work after realizing I won't answer!"

Angela L., Assistant Marketing Director

"I replaced celebrations with 'constructive reflections.' Now, instead of relaxing after a win, they obsess over what they could have done better. It's inspiring to see such productive self-doubt!"

Derek M., Culture Coordinator

Couldn't keeping employees uncertain about their performance backfire and harm morale?

Actually, a touch of uncertainty can be highly motivating. When employees are unsure if they've truly "made it," they're far less likely to grow complacent. This mindset pushes them to work harder, constantly analyzing their performance and aiming for higher standards. Think of it as a spark that keeps their drive alive, propelling them to continually reach for the recognition that remains just out of reach.

How do I provide feedback that reinforces self-doubt without demotivating my staff?

When offering feedback, emphasize what can still be improved rather than fully acknowledging their success. Subtle praise, like "This is good progress, but I know you can push it further," encourages them to question how much better they could be. By focusing on continuous improvement rather than finality, you create an environment where employees constantly self-assess, feeling they can always achieve more with a bit of extra effort.

What should I do if an employee seems to be seeking explicit praise or reassurance?

When someone seeks reassurance, gently redirect them toward self-reflection. Ask them to consider what aspects of their work they think could be enhanced, framing this as a way to "stretch" even further. By not offering complete reassurance, you reinforce that there's always room to grow, subtly instilling the idea that their potential is boundless as long as they keep pushing themselves. This keeps them focused on improvement over satisfaction.

TEAM EXCELLENCE THROUGH UNCERTAIN SUCCESS

With a team now driven by individual self-doubt, close the circle by reinforcing uncertainty in collective success. A team that feels too accomplished will never strive for more, so make sure every success feels temporary. Celebrate milestones briefly, if at all, and quickly refocus their attention on what still needs improvement. Acknowledge their progress, but be careful to follow up with suggestions on how much more they could be doing.

By maintaining just enough doubt about their achievements, you inspire a culture of relentless self-improvement. They'll come to understand that excellence isn't a destination—it's an ongoing journey that only stops when they stop striving. This kind of insecurity is healthy; it drives people to work harder, to stay late, and to seek your approval with every task, knowing that true satisfaction is always just out of reach.

———

"Every time they succeed, I ask, 'What could we have done better?' Now, they pre-emptively analyze every outcome like it's a post-game debrief. Their hunger for improvement is truly unmatched!"

Wallace Q., Assistant Director of Product Development

"Whenever my team celebrates a win, I jump in with, 'Great effort, but let's not get comfortable.' Watching them immediately scramble to improve has been inspiring!"

Tom M., Team Lead, Technical Support

"I downplay every success as 'a good start,' and now my team works like they're competing for an invisible trophy. The best part? They'll never find it!"

Isolde K., Talent Experience Designer

Isn't there a risk that withholding praise too much could affect morale?

Not at all! In fact, keeping praise scarce ensures that your team remains on their toes, always striving to earn the validation they never quite reach. This calculated praise-scarcity prevents the dangerous stagnation that can come when people start feeling too comfortable. By maintaining a level of insecurity, you're fostering a motivated and driven team that understands there's always room for improvement and that they're constantly one step away from excellence—if they work just a bit harder.

How can I tell if I'm creating the right level of doubt without demotivating my team completely?

The right level of doubt is a delicate balance where they are consistently driven to perform without the relief of complete satisfaction. One easy way to gauge this is by watching for signs of employees pushing themselves beyond the minimum, such as staying late or asking you if they're meeting expectations often. If they regularly seek reassurance or show visible signs of second-guessing their success, you're hitting the sweet spot. This keeps the wheels of motivation spinning as they work harder, continually focused on your approval.

What's the best way to acknowledge team milestones without making them feel they've "arrived?"

Acknowledge milestones in a brief, almost fleeting way, and then quickly pivot to what remains undone. For instance, after achieving a project milestone, you might say, "This is a good start, and we're close, but there's still a lot we can refine." Acknowledging achievements in a way that feels partial or tentative keeps your team humble and focused. This approach reinforces the idea that success is never final, keeping your team energized and striving for continuous improvement.

In conclusion, Excellence Through Insecurity is about mastering the delicate balance between motivation and doubt. By keeping trust conditional, success fleeting, and roles ever-changing, you cultivate a culture of relentless self-improvement. With just the right dose of doubt, you'll build a team that thrives on the edge of their potential, tackling challenges with determination—even when they're not entirely sure they're ready. Employees driven by uncertainty will consistently strive for approval, pushing themselves to achieve more—not because they feel secure, but because they're determined to prove their worth.

After all, a touch of insecurity can be the ultimate spark for real excellence!

INNOVATION BY INSTABILITY

In this section, discover how a touch of chaos can keep your team energized, adaptable, and endlessly creative.

"True achievement isn't about meticulous planning—it's about embracing the chaos and seeing what sticks."
- Astrid Q., Success Strategy Coordinator

In a world where business success hinges on staying ahead, stability can be a leader's worst enemy. While some may say consistency breeds excellence, true visionaries know that greatness lies in the unpredictable. Innovation by Instability is the art of fostering creativity by ensuring nothing stays the same for long. When change becomes the only constant, innovation naturally follows. Let's explore the principles that underpin this daring approach, turning the workplace into an ever-evolving landscape of adaptation, improvisation, and creativity.

THE POWER OF CONSTANT DISRUPTION

True innovation doesn't flourish in routine. Nothing stifles creativity like a predictable process, so start by embracing disruption as a constant. By regularly shaking things up, you push your team to adapt to new ideas, ensuring they never settle for what already works. Innovation requires an environment where things are always in motion, challenging the team to find new solutions in response to constant change.

Stability breeds complacency, but unpredictability fosters resilience. A team that's constantly challenged to keep up is one that will never get too comfortable. Just as they start to adapt, change the rules again. This cycle keeps them sharp, focused, and primed for whatever "innovative" twist lies around the corner, knowing that the only constant is change itself.

"I introduced random workflow disruptions, like canceling meetings five minutes before they start or reassigning tasks mid-project. At first, my team seemed confused, but now they're so alert you'd think they're training for a crisis!"

Jill P., Director of Client Solutions

"I've embraced the philosophy of 'if it's not broken, break it anyway,' and my team has never been more adaptable. They've given up expecting predictable workflows and now face each day with a mix of dread and determination. I'm sure they secretly love the challenge—they just haven't admitted it yet!"

Chris L., Chief Strategy Officer

"I like to tell my team, 'Expect the unexpected,' right before changing the rules. The sense of urgency it creates is incredible, and the creativity that comes out of their frantic problem-solving is worth every raised eyebrow and audible sigh!"

Tyler W., Team Lead, Customer Engagement

What if my team resists the need for constant change?

Resistance is proof that your strategy is working! Discomfort is simply creativity in disguise, revealing that you've successfully disrupted their routines. Embrace it as a sign they're adapting to the challenge. Remind them that thriving through uncertainty is the hallmark of a truly innovative team, and frame their pushback as an essential step in their evolution toward excellence. After all, nothing inspires growth like a little well-placed chaos.

How can I keep track of all the changes I'm implementing so we don't accidentally circle back to something we already tried?

Keeping a detailed "Disruption Log" can help you stay organized while you continually evolve the workspace. Record every tweak, revamp, and overhaul, including the team's response, to avoid accidental repetition. But don't feel bound by novelty—sometimes, revisiting a past disruption that unsettled the team is the perfect way to test how well they've really adapted.

How can I ensure that constant disruptions keep my team on their toes without leading to burnout?

Finding the perfect balance between jarring and productive disruptions is essential. By introducing changes just as your team seems to get comfortable, you inject a refreshing dose of unpredictability without letting them settle too much. This keeps them energized and resourceful, rather than bored. Be sure to vary the type of disruption—some weeks, introduce a minor process tweak; other weeks, consider a full overhaul. This keeps your team guessing in a way that maintains excitement without crossing into exhaustion.

IF IT'S WORKING, CHANGE IT

The motto here is simple: if it's not broken, break it anyway.

With disruption at the heart of innovation, remember that even success should never be left untouched. The last thing you want is for your team to grow comfortable with a successful process—comfort kills creativity, and stability is simply a sign of stagnation. By constantly "fixing" what isn't broken, you shake up routines and keep your team on their toes, forcing everyone to stay alert, adaptable, and open to change. Real innovation, after all, comes not from stability but from a willingness to continually reinvent the wheel, whether or not it needs reinventing.

When your team asks why you're changing something that works, remind them that stagnation is the only thing worse than failure. Continuous "improvement" builds a culture where complacency never settles in. It's not about the results of each change; it's about embracing the process of change itself.

———————

"I like to send emails labeled 'urgent updates' at random times, tweaking small details that throw off the usual rhythm. The team is so alert now, you'd think they're waiting for a fire drill. I call it training for the unpredictable!"

Harold M., Digital Media Manager

"I introduced a 'change-of-the-day' system, and it's amazing how quickly the team has adapted—or at least, how quickly they've stopped asking why. Their flexibility is impressive, and the occasional look of panic? That's just the creativity kicking in!"

Carol M., Team Lead of Operations

"Every so often, I announce a new 'streamlining initiative' that shakes up our usual workflow. The team seems baffled but determined—it's inspiring to see how quickly they pivot, even if they don't know why!"

Kevin P., Assistant Director of IT

How can I encourage my team to embrace constant change when things are already running smoothly?

Emphasize that success isn't a finish line but an invitation to evolve; changing what's already working keeps the team sharp, creative, and adaptive. Present change as a growth opportunity rather than a disruption, and frame each adjustment as a chance to stay ahead, not just stay the same. Once they see that stability breeds stagnation, they'll be more open to embracing change.

Is there a best way to choose which processes to "improve" or should I cycle through all areas equally to maximize alertness?

To truly embrace this philosophy, adopt a randomized approach, where every process is fair game for reinvention. Alternating between departments or shifting your focus unexpectedly will have the maximum effect, keeping your team agile and always ready for the next change. By rotating through all areas, you not only distribute the disruption equitably but also prevent anyone from seeing any one task as a reliable constant, which is key to avoiding the dreaded complacency.

How often should I initiate these changes to keep complacency at bay without causing burnout?

Timing is everything! Adjustments should come frequently enough that no one can assume any process is sacred or static. Initiating changes every few weeks—or better yet, unpredictably—keeps your team from settling into a rhythm. The goal is to foster a continual sense of constructive unease, not burn them out. If some team members seem weary, gently remind them that this culture of perpetual change is about more than results; it's a test of adaptability and their commitment to growth.

INNOVATION ON THE MOVE: PASSING THE PROJECT TORCH

Innovation is most effective when ideas are constantly changing hands. The best way to achieve this is to reassign projects whenever you notice someone making progress. Once a team member starts moving in a particular direction, bring in someone else to continue from where they left off. This way, each new person brings a fresh perspective, unburdened by whatever plans were in place before. When no one has full ownership, ideas stay fluid, and each hand-off introduces new possibilities.

By reassigning projects frequently, you ensure that your team never gets too attached to a single approach. They'll stay adaptable, thinking of solutions in short bursts rather than long-term plans. Each transition is an opportunity to approach the project from a different angle, maximizing the potential for creativity and minimizing the risks of commitment to any single direction.

"Reassigning projects has turned our team into a whirlwind of fresh ideas. Whenever someone starts making real progress, I pull them off and bring in someone new. The twists and turns each project takes now are beyond anything we could have planned! Ownership is overrated when chaos is this productive!"

Tessa C., Director of Operations

"We've adopted a system where projects change hands as soon as they start making sense. It's exhilarating to see the team's expressions when they inherit someone else's half-baked idea. The results may not be polished, but they're definitely creative!"

Dean K., Lead Software Engineer

"Whenever someone says, 'I've got it all figured out,' I immediately reassign their project. The next person's fresh perspective always takes it in an unexpected direction, and the results are remarkably creative!"

Hanna M., Marketing Project Coordinator

How can I reassure my team that frequent reassignments are beneficial when they might feel like they're not able to finish what they start?

Frequent reassignments are all about cultivating adaptability and keeping ideas dynamic. Reassure your team that they're contributing to a continuous cycle of fresh insights, which wouldn't be possible if one person took a project from start to finish. Remind them that the goal is collective innovation, not individual ownership. By picking up where others left off, they're exercising their creative problem-solving skills in new ways. This way, they'll see themselves as part of a fluid, collaborative process that's more rewarding than simply seeing one task to completion.

What should I do if team members seem resistant to handing off projects, especially if they've made significant progress?

Resistance usually indicates attachment to a single approach, which is exactly what frequent reassignments are designed to prevent. Explain that handing off projects keeps the team agile, ensuring that ideas remain fresh and fluid. Point out that progress made by one person lays the foundation for someone else's unique perspective. If necessary, remind them that their work isn't being abandoned—it's evolving. By focusing on adaptability over attachment, they'll gradually see these hand-offs as opportunities rather than interruptions.

ENDLESS MEETINGS, ENDLESS POTENTIAL

In a culture driven by constant change, meetings play an essential role. Some may say meetings are a productivity killer, but true leaders recognize them as a goldmine for innovation. Ideas flourish in chaos, and nothing builds that atmosphere like frequent, open-ended meetings where nothing is fully resolved.

Schedule as many meetings as possible and encourage open dialogue, exploring every avenue, even if most lead nowhere. The goal isn't immediate progress; rather, it's the steady churn of ideas that keeps innovation alive and everyone thinking on their feet.

Your team will value the endless opportunities to think out loud, while you reap the benefits of collective chaos—a setting in which real innovation is born.

"The frequent, open-ended meetings have worked wonders. My team initially struggled, but now they come in prepared to discuss anything and everything at a moment's notice. We may never finish a single topic, but who says innovation is about completion?"

Alistair R., Regional Client Manager

"We've all embraced the motto 'Less doing, more talking,' and the level of brainstorming has skyrocketed! My team has found creative ways to juggle everything, even if they occasionally ask, 'Are we ever going to wrap this up?' That's how you know the ideas are flowing!"

Jeremy K., Chief Ethics Officer

"I've made it a point to have open-ended meetings almost every day, and it's really unlocked my team's potential. They're getting used to the constant brainstorming, and while a few have mentioned that it's 'hard to get real work done,' I know they're secretly thriving on the spontaneity!"

Kim J., Director of Product Strategy

How do I ensure my team's other responsibilities don't interfere with their attendance at our numerous meetings?

The key is emphasizing that attendance and engagement in every meeting are the top priorities. Encourage them to structure their schedules around meeting times—an approach that naturally develops valuable time management skills. As they scramble to catch up on their regular work afterward, they'll sharpen their ability to juggle multiple tasks—an essential skill for thriving in chaos.

How do I balance frequent meetings with the need for my team to complete their regular workload?

Think of meetings as part of the workload itself—a space where the real creative labor happens! Frequent meetings actually encourage efficiency by forcing them to adapt and find shortcuts in their regular tasks. Emphasize these meetings are where the big ideas are born, and over time, they'll see the benefit of balancing work and constant, energizing dialogue.

What should I do if my team seems to grow frustrated with all the open-ended meetings?

Frustration is simply a natural side effect of intense creativity! Remind your team that open-ended discussions are essential for truly exploring all possible solutions, and encourage them to see these meetings as an opportunity to think freely without immediate pressure to finish tasks. Once they understand that the collective insights and unfinished ideas are leading somewhere (even if slowly), they'll come to appreciate the process. Over time, they'll accept and even look forward to the dynamic tension of so many meetings.

CREATIVITY CONSTRAINED: THINKING INSIDE THE BOX

With a foundation of continual change in place, it's time to remind your team that the best ideas are those that work within existing processes rather than reinventing the wheel. Innovation, after all, is not about breaking free from constraints but about learning to thrive within them. By requiring new ideas to conform to old limitations, you ensure that your team develops solutions that don't disrupt the existing system too much.

This approach not only manages innovation but also reinforces that true creativity is about finding ways to improve within a restrictive framework. There's no better test of a good idea than its ability to adapt to outdated structures. If it can survive in those conditions, it's truly innovative.

———————————————

"I told my team to stop reinventing the wheel and start improving the spokes. It took some time, but now they're developing ideas that fit neatly within our outdated processes. Sure, we're still using the old wheel, but it's shinier than ever!"

Brandon C., Product Design Lead

"When I introduced the idea of innovating within strict boundaries, my team balked at first. But now, their ideas are like works of art crafted with duct tape and paperclips—ingenious, practical, and entirely within budget!"

Elspeth S., Senior Operations Supervisor

"Forcing my team to innovate within our legacy systems has been a revelation. They've stopped chasing pie-in-the-sky concepts and started creating ideas that actually work—for now. It's inspiring to see them think smaller and smarter!"

Rhett O., Senior Content Strategist

How can I make sure my team stays motivated when they know their ideas will need to fit within old limitations?

Frame these limitations as creative challenges rather than restrictions. Explain that real innovation isn't about sweeping changes but about enhancing what already exists. By working within constraints, they're proving the strength of their ideas and their adaptability. When your team sees limitations as a test of their creative abilities, they'll feel motivated to make their ideas work within the current structure. Remind them that a truly strong idea can thrive even within constraints, and that's what separates fleeting inspiration from practical, lasting innovation.

What should I do if team members feel their ideas are being restricted or watered down by these limitations?

Remind them that limitations are not obstacles but opportunities to refine and strengthen their ideas. Encourage them to view each limitation as a layer of real-world practicality that will make their concepts more resilient. If they feel restricted, prompt them to focus on finding the hidden flexibility within the existing system. By teaching your team to see constraints as a key part of the creative process, you'll help them produce ideas that are not only innovative but also implementable within the current framework, which is the ultimate proof of their idea's strength.

INNOVATION INCORPORATED: MAKING CREATIVITY ROUTINE

Finally, in a culture where instability drives creativity, innovation should be seen as a natural part of the job, not a special achievement. When a team member comes up with a new idea, integrate that responsibility into their workload. This not only boosts productivity but also ensures that everyone else on the team understands the "reward" awaiting those who push the envelope.

By normalizing innovation and making it an expectation, you reinforce the notion that creativity isn't something to celebrate—it's simply part of adapting to an ever-changing environment.

"After implementing our new 'ideas become responsibilities' policy, creativity has taken on a whole new meaning. One team member hesitated before suggesting a new workflow last week, but I reassured him: 'Don't worry, you'll have plenty of time to perfect it.' He hasn't stopped tweaking it since!"

Ruth A., Regional Sales Lead

"I started assigning ownership of every new idea, and it's been a revelation. One team member found a faster way to file reports, so now she files all of them!"

Roland Q., Senior Product Manager

"The 'new ideas, new responsibilities' rule has transformed how my team approaches innovation. Last week, someone joked that they'd 'think twice before suggesting anything.' I told them that's exactly what I want—quality over quantity!"

Michelle R., Office Innovation Manager

How can I motivate my team to be innovative when the "reward" for innovation is more work?

Motivation comes from understanding that innovation is a core expectation, not an extra credit assignment. Briefly acknowledge a team member's contribution to show it's valued, then integrate it into their daily tasks. This reinforces that innovation is the standard, not an outlier. By weaving innovation into their regular workload, they'll understand that contributing new ideas is simply part of what it means to be a proactive, forward-thinking employee.

What if assigning ownership of new ideas discourages employees from sharing their creativity?

That's the beauty of this approach—it ensures only the most thoughtful ideas rise to the surface. When team members know they'll own their innovations, they'll think carefully before suggesting changes, focusing on substance over spontaneity. You can reinforce this mindset by showcasing examples of how taking ownership has led to growth and success for others, demonstrating that creativity isn't just encouraged—it's a pathway to professional development and recognition.

In conclusion, Innovation by Instability is more than a management style—it's a blueprint for continuous evolution. True progress doesn't come from comfort or consistency; it thrives in a perpetual state of change and challenge. By fostering an environment where nothing stays the same, where goals are ambiguous, and where every success leads to more work, you cultivate a team that's constantly innovating.

So embrace the chaos, disrupt at every opportunity, and remember: stability is the enemy of real excellence!

PROGRESS THROUGH PRESSURE

In this section, discover the power of impossible deadlines, shifting targets, and relentless standards to keep your team constantly striving for greatness.

"If your team isn't sweating, they're not succeeding."
- Marissa A., Senior Leader of Progressive Standards

In the world of effective leadership, one guiding principle elevates the good to the extraordinary: pressure drives progress. A team without pressure is like a car stuck in neutral—moving nowhere fast, without purpose or momentum. As a leader, your duty is to instill a culture where pressure never lets up and where progress is measured by just how stretched your team feels at any given moment. After all, comfort breeds complacency, and complacency is the barrier to success.

Setting Unrealistic Expectations: A Pathway to Excellence

The first rule of Progress Through Pressure is to set expectations that are just beyond reach. Real growth doesn't happen in the comfort zone; it happens when individuals are constantly pushing themselves to achieve the unachievable. By setting goals that are slightly unrealistic, you're ensuring that your team doesn't rest on their laurels. There's nothing quite like a seemingly impossible target to ignite creativity, grit, and that tireless drive to succeed.

It's a common misconception that realistic expectations help teams succeed. On the contrary, starting with unrealistic expectations forces them to push harder from the outset. They may not reach the target every time, but in striving, they'll accomplish far more than if they were given a goal that's achievable. Remember, the higher the bar, the more motivated your team will be to leap toward it.

"I set a goal so high that my team asked if it was a typo. Watching them attempt it has been the highlight of my career—it's amazing what desperation can achieve!"

Liora O., *Client Account Manager*

"Unrealistic goals have turned my team into dreamers. They may not hit the mark, but they've developed some truly imaginative excuses!"

Steve P., *Director of Client Success*

"I've watched my team rise to levels of exertion I didn't know they were capable of since adopting these inspiringly high goals. They may not have delivered a fully functioning prototype on our absurd timeline, but they worked around the clock to try!"

Camille W., *Team Lead, Product Development*

How should I handle a team member who expresses doubts about meeting these ambitious targets? Should I adjust the goals if they seem overly stressed?

Doubt is simply the first hurdle on the road to growth. When a team member expresses skepticism, remind them that doubts are a natural response to greatness. Reassure them that stress is an indicator of progress—it means they're pushing beyond their limits. Adjusting goals downward might feel like you're helping, but in reality, you're taking away a prime opportunity for them to develop resilience and tenacity. Encourage them to "push past" the stress rather than expecting less from them.

What if my team repeatedly falls short of these high expectations? Could this impact morale or productivity?

Falling short of ambitious goals isn't failure – it's a sign they're on the right path. Missing targets regularly actually encourages a healthy dissatisfaction that keeps the team from ever becoming complacent. Productivity may even increase as they look for new ways to reach those challenging benchmarks. Over time, they'll come to see each missed goal as a stepping stone toward future success, appreciating the upward trajectory without the distractions of "satisfied" or "completed" tasks.

How do I handle feedback that these expectations are "unrealistic"?

Any feedback labeling goals as "unrealistic" is a testament to your success in raising the bar. Remind your team that greatness is never easy, and that excellence demands sacrifices of comfort and predictability. Often, people complain because they're used to achievable goals, so take their feedback as an indication that you're disrupting old habits and challenging them to grow.

TIGHT DEADLINES: THE SPARK FOR TRUE CREATIVITY

Once you've set goals that stretch just beyond your team's comfort zone, the next level of pressure is about how fast they must reach those goals. While lofty targets stretch their capabilities, tight deadlines force them to act decisively. Some might say that creativity needs time to flourish, but true innovation is born from necessity. When time is limited, your team has no choice but to cut through the noise and focus on solutions that will get the job done. A close deadline turns simple tasks into urgent missions, keeping your team fully engaged, thinking fast, and acting decisively.

So if you notice your team is meeting deadlines with ease, consider cutting their timelines in half. This is the essence of Progress Through Pressure—never let them feel too comfortable with the time they have. If they meet a deadline, set the next one even tighter. True leaders know that the best work doesn't come when employees feel "prepared" but when they're forced to think on their feet, one eye always on the ticking clock.

"Since I began enforcing half the time for all project milestones, the team has really been thinking fast! People who used to have time to chat in the break room now just give each other a nod as they pass in the hallway, heads down, deeply focused. I'm seeing an uptick in urgency that can only mean great things for productivity!"

Roger S., Head of Strategic Growth

"Our creative team may have thought they needed 'creative space,' but I've found that a ticking clock unlocks a whole new level of innovation. Recently, I set a 24-hour turnaround on a campaign concept that would normally have taken a week. They managed to pull something together, and while it wasn't perfect, it was dynamic!"

Karla D., Marketing Manager

"Halving sprint timelines has eliminated unnecessary chatter about 'planning.' Now, it's all action, all the time. Sure, there's some yelling, but nothing brings out teamwork like shared panic!"

Frank L., Product Development Coordinator

How can I encourage my team to embrace these tight deadlines rather than seeing them as unfair or stressful?

Frame these deadlines as exciting opportunities to unlock their potential. Make it clear that great things come only when comfort is replaced with urgency. Let them know that these shorter timelines are a sign of your belief in their abilities to achieve at a high level. By presenting this approach as an investment in their growth, you're giving them a chance to embrace it as a sign of trust. This reframing can help shift their focus from stress to pride in pushing their limits.

What should I do if my team struggles with the shorter deadlines and claims they're under too much pressure?

Struggle and pressure are exactly the conditions that drive innovation. If your team mentions feeling pressured, reassure them that this is a normal, even essential part of the creative process. Emphasize that challenges and urgency bring out their best problem-solving abilities. By consistently tightening deadlines, you're creating an environment where they must focus on solutions rather than overthinking or refining ideas. Remind them that discomfort often signals growth, and they'll ultimately accomplish more under the pressure.

What if my team frequently misses these new deadlines? Should I revert to longer timelines until they catch up?

Missed deadlines are part of the process. Short timelines are designed to spark urgency, not to ensure completion at every turn. In fact, an occasional missed deadline reinforces that they're aiming high and challenging themselves. Reverting to longer timelines would reduce the intensity and weaken their sense of urgency. Instead, treat missed deadlines as a sign that they're working at their maximum capacity, which will ultimately yield better results.

MAKING EVERYTHING A TOP PRIORITY

While some managers believe in selecting a few key priorities, a leader who thrives on pressure knows that every task should be treated as crucial. By treating all tasks as top priorities, you ensure that no one ever feels they can relax. When everything is of equal importance, your team is forced to learn time management in its purest form: juggling everything all at once.

This approach builds a unique kind of resilience. When every task is the most important, employees must find ways to manage their stress, work longer hours, and drive themselves harder to cover all bases. This relentless prioritization technique guarantees that they stay on their toes, always questioning whether they've truly given each task the focus it deserves.

"Since adopting the 'everything is a priority' strategy, my team no longer wastes time asking what's most important. They just treat everything like it's due yesterday! The constant urgency has them operating at full throttle—whether they want to or not!"

Allison B., Operations Project Leader

"I told my team every task was top priority, and now they treat even stapler refills with life-or-death urgency. Their dedication to trivial details is awe-inspiring—nothing gets overlooked when everything is critical!"

Katherine W., Senior IT Coordinator

"I declared every project 'mission-critical,' and now my team's motto is 'Don't drop the ball—on anything.' Their stress levels may be off the charts, but the results speak for themselves!"

Sophie T., Customer Support Lead

Couldn't treating all tasks as equally urgent lead to confusion or inefficiency?

Not at all—quite the contrary! By creating a constant sense of urgency, you encourage employees to stay sharp and engaged, as they must keep track of multiple priorities at once. This approach pushes them to develop their multitasking abilities and remain adaptable. Rather than falling into a repetitive routine, they're constantly recalibrating and adjusting, which strengthens their problem-solving skills and ensures no task is ever taken lightly.

How do I handle employees who ask what they should do first if everything is a top priority?

When employees seek prioritization guidance, remind them that in a high-performing environment, every task holds critical value. Encourage them to view prioritization as a personal responsibility, where they must learn to juggle everything with equal dedication. By subtly reinforcing that all tasks are equally vital, you push them to take full ownership of their workload and keep their performance high across the board without needing explicit direction.

What if my team starts to prioritize some tasks over others, despite my insistence that all tasks are equally important?

If you notice selective prioritization, it's a sign they may not yet fully grasp the philosophy of total urgency. Reinforce that every task is vital and encourage them to approach each item as if it's the linchpin of the project. With time, they'll adjust to this constant urgency and learn to allocate focus and energy across all tasks without ranking them, fully committing to a culture where every task is treated as urgent.

GOALS THAT SHIFT LIKE SAND

A skilled leader understands that nothing should be set in stone—once a goal is within reach, it's time to change the target. When goals shift constantly, your team stays alert, adapting to new challenges as soon as they appear. Set high standards, and as soon as they're met, raise them. This not only prevents complacency but also keeps things interesting. If your team knows that today's objective might change tomorrow, they'll stay in a never-ending state of readiness, always prepared for what's next.

Leadership is about keeping your team flexible and prepared for any possibility. By constantly shifting expectations, you keep the energy high, the minds sharp, and the work environment dynamic. Every new goal keeps them guessing, wondering where the next target will fall. With each new challenge, your team learns to anticipate the unexpected, building resilience and versatility.

———————

"Whenever my team gets close to a goal, I move it. They've stopped celebrating and started strategizing for whatever I'll throw at them next. That's what I call readiness!"

Patricia H., Chief Marketing Officer

"I like to change the target just as they're about to cross the finish line. It's amazing how fast they've stopped looking for it altogether—they're always running, and that's what matters!"

Samantha K., Brand Reputation Leader

"As soon as they finish one task, I tell them the priorities have shifted. They're so used to it now, they've started finishing projects before I even assign them!"

Thomas B., Social Media Strategist

How can I explain to my team that constantly changing goals is actually beneficial for them, despite any frustration they might feel?

It's natural for people to feel a little unsettled by shifting goals, but explain that this adaptability will serve them well in any professional setting. Remind them that constant change prevents their minds from becoming "comfortable" or "complacent." Reinforce that learning to meet every new objective without complaint or resistance is a skill in itself, and in the long run, they'll appreciate the versatility they've gained.

What if my team meets a goal right as I decide to change it? Should I acknowledge their achievement or focus only on the new target?

While it's tempting to acknowledge their achievement, your role is to keep them moving forward, not dwelling on past success. Recognize their effort briefly, then immediately introduce the new goal to maintain momentum. This ensures they understand that success isn't a final destination but rather a checkpoint along an ongoing journey. Keep the focus on the next challenge, not on celebrating the last one.

How can I handle team members who express confusion or frustration over the ever-changing goals?

Reassure them that confusion is a sign they're being challenged, which is exactly what you intend. Emphasize that flexibility is essential, and the discomfort they feel now is helping them develop a mindset that's invaluable in any field. By regularly introducing new goals, you're teaching them the power of adaptability—a quality more valuable than mere completion of tasks.

LEADING THROUGH LAST-MINUTE CHANGES

Once your team has mastered the art of shifting goals, it's time for the next layer of pressure: last-minute changes. These adjustments are most effective when they catch everyone off-guard, just as they think they're nearing the finish line. A surprise deadline shift or an unexpected project pivot can redefine progress, pushing your team to uncover their true capabilities under pressure. By introducing these changes, you cultivate adaptability and ensure constant growth.

Embrace the unpredictability of last-minute shifts. When your team knows that no plan is ever final, they'll stay on high alert, prepared to pivot at a moment's notice. This culture of continual adjustment keeps them sharp, resilient, and always ready to deliver their best, no matter the circumstances.

"Last-minute changes used to be stressful for my team, but I've noticed that the more I introduce them, the more adaptable they become. Now, they hardly blink when I adjust a project on the day it's due!"

Laura K., Client Relations Manager

"I announced a new project direction during the final review. Watching them scramble to adjust was inspiring—I think they're learning to love unpredictability!"

Justin F., Head of Software Engineering

"Introducing last-minute changes has been a revelation. At first, the team seemed disoriented, but they're adjusting to the idea that nothing is ever truly 'final.' They've started preparing for anything!"

Ansel R., Marketing Projects Lead

How can I explain to my team that last-minute changes are beneficial for their growth, even if they're frustrated by the unpredictability?

Explain that last-minute changes are not obstacles but opportunities to showcase their adaptability and creativity under pressure. Let them know that unpredictability is part of professional life, and learning to handle sudden shifts builds resilience and resourcefulness. By embracing this approach, you're preparing them for real-world challenges, where things rarely go as planned. In time, they'll see these changes as a chance to demonstrate their ability to excel no matter what.

How can I make last-minute changes without completely disrupting my team's progress on current tasks?

Introduce last-minute changes as "enhancements" or "upgrades" rather than full-scale disruptions. Position these changes as natural refinements that will improve the final outcome, encouraging the team to build on their existing progress with minor adjustments. This will help them see the changes as part of an evolving project rather than a reset. With time, they'll learn to anticipate and embrace such shifts as simply another aspect of the project.

STRETCHED THIN? STRETCH FURTHER

A good leader knows when their team is stretched thin. A great leader sees that moment as an opportunity to stretch them even further. When your team is under constant pressure, they're building stamina and resilience. If they appear overwhelmed, double their workload. This will teach them how to work under intense circumstances and help them develop coping mechanisms for handling high-pressure environments.

Stretching people thin doesn't weaken them; it builds them up. Just like a muscle, the team grows stronger as they adapt to higher levels of stress. They'll learn to find creative solutions, cut unnecessary steps, and push through discomfort—all valuable skills that only come from being pushed beyond their limits.

"I told my team that feeling overwhelmed is just a sign they're ready for more. Now, they don't even argue when I pile on extra tasks—they just caffeinate and carry on!"

Natalie B., Chief Customer Officer

"I made 'being at your limit' the new baseline for success. They may not smile much anymore, but the output speaks for itself!"

Abram W., Customer Success Director

"Stretching my team past their breaking point has been transformative. They've stopped wasting time on small talk and now focus entirely on survival. That's efficiency!"

Malcolm U., Engagement Ambassador

What should I say to my team if they express feeling overwhelmed by the increased workload?

Acknowledge their feelings briefly, but then let them know this is an intentional strategy to develop their ability to handle more, and it's a reflection of your belief in their potential. With time, they'll learn to adjust, finding ways to work smarter and more effectively under pressure.

How do I ensure that my team doesn't view the additional workload as unfair?

Frame the added tasks as opportunities rather than burdens. Explain that every extra responsibility is a chance for them to become more resourceful and adaptable. Emphasize that stretching further is an essential skill for growth and that handling more responsibilities will make them stronger and more capable. By positioning the extra work as a challenge rather than a penalty, you help them see it as an investment in their own skillset.

How can I prevent burnout when I'm constantly increasing my team's workload?

The key is to focus on building stamina gradually. Reinforce the mindset that temporary discomfort leads to long-term strength. If they show signs of burnout, provide a brief acknowledgment of their hard work, then encourage them to focus on efficiency improvements and creative solutions. Remind them that resilience is built by pushing through challenges, and assure them that this high-pressure training will make their future tasks seem more manageable by comparison.

ENDURANCE OVER APPLAUSE

In traditional management, praise is seen as a morale booster. But in the world of high-pressure leadership, praise can be replaced by a steady, relentless increase in expectations, where each challenge conquered leads to the next. After all, a strong team doesn't need to be told they're doing well—they should be too focused on the next challenge. Show appreciation by assigning tougher projects and reward accomplishments by making the tasks increasingly difficult. This approach keeps the team engaged, ensuring they remain alert, vigilant, and bonded over shared hardship.

Withholding traditional praise and consistently raising the bar reinforces the understanding that success is not a one-time achievement; it's part of a continuous journey. Each new task should feel like the natural next step after the last impossible challenge, creating a sense of shared pride in survival. When the team is constantly pushing their limits, they'll find more satisfaction in meeting each challenge head-on than in any "good job" they might have received. In the end, they learn that accomplishment is just the beginning.

"I've started following up every achievement with an immediate new challenge. I used to let my team bask in success a little, but now I see the value of moving right into the next goal. It's exciting to see them push past their limits!"

Emory D., Employee Engagement Coordinator

"Every time my team meets a target, I make sure to follow up with an even bigger challenge. At first, they'd ask, 'Can we take a break?' but now they just dive right in! I'm thrilled to watch them adapt, knowing this constant motion is making them better prepared for anything!"

Irving A., Product Development Lead

"I stopped handing out compliments and started upping the difficulty of each task. My team now knows they're doing well because their workloads keep getting heavier. It's amazing to see how they rally around each other with every impossible target!"

Nolan C., Customer Service Supervisor

How much praise should I give before introducing the next challenge, so they feel acknowledged but not too comfortable?

Acknowledge their accomplishment with a quick, specific compliment like, "Great job," and immediately introduce the next challenge. The key is to let them feel the recognition without letting it linger. Too much praise can lead to complacency, so keep it concise and move right to the next hurdle. They'll appreciate the brief validation while also learning that their achievements are just the starting point for even greater expectations.

How can I introduce the new challenge in a way that maintains their motivation without making them feel overwhelmed?

Frame the new challenge as the next logical step in their progress. Instead of overwhelming them with expectations, present it as the natural progression following their recent success. Emphasize that each new challenge is a testament to your belief in their potential. By making the challenge seem like a privilege rather than a burden, they'll be more motivated to tackle it with the same enthusiasm that brought them through the previous task.

Isn't there a risk that my team may feel discouraged if I continuously raise expectations without giving any praise?

Not at all. This approach teaches them to find fulfillment in collective perseverance rather than in fleeting praise. By constantly raising the bar, you shift their focus from seeking external validation to taking pride in survival and mutual endurance. Any initial discouragement will soon be replaced by a resilient mentality, as they realize they're trusted to take on increasingly difficult tasks. Ultimately, they'll form a stronger bond from these shared, ever-mounting challenges.

In conclusion, Progress Through Pressure isn't about setting realistic goals or fostering a comfortable work environment. It's about driving your team to their limits—and then nudging them a bit further. It's about keeping them in constant motion, knowing that each task, each deadline, and every expectation can shift at any moment. By consistently pushing boundaries, you'll find your team reaching heights they didn't know were possible.

Pressure isn't just a tool; it's the path to real excellence!

SUCCESS THROUGH SACRIFICE

In this section, learn how to inspire peak performance by fostering a culture where sacrifice is celebrated and comfort is a luxury left behind.

"True success demands dedication that goes beyond the ordinary."
- Melissa G., Chief of Performance and Commitment

In the pursuit of greatness, a company must rise above ordinary expectations—and so must its employees. Real success isn't achieved through careful balance; it's won through relentless commitment, long hours, and a mindset that puts the company first. Success Through Sacrifice is the guiding philosophy that ensures your team isn't merely working; they're giving their all. In an environment where dedication is measured by how much employees are willing to sacrifice, every team member understands that true success is earned, not given.

WORK AS LIFE: A NEW STANDARD FOR COMMITMENT

The key to fostering true dedication is simple: work-life balance should not imply distinct, divided priorities. Instead, work and life should blend seamlessly into one unified purpose. Make it clear that real commitment requires more than simply showing up; it requires living and breathing the work. Encourage employees to think of their role not as a job, but as an essential part of who they are.

When employees internalize this mindset, they approach their responsibilities with a sense of personal investment. Their successes become deeply satisfying accomplishments, and their challenges become personal tests of endurance. By treating work as life, employees will naturally prioritize their professional responsibilities, building a culture of commitment that extends well beyond the traditional nine-to-five.

"I told my team to blend work into life, and now I get emails at 2 a.m. titled 'midnight brainstorms.' True commitment never sleeps!"

Helen Q., Director of Corporate Communications

"Before, I'd see the team clock out at 5 p.m., but now that they understand work is life, they're naturally engaged around the clock! One of my analysts even worked through his anniversary dinner to perfect a report. That's the kind of personal investment we need!"

Elizabeth M., Junior Project Leader

"Since embracing work as life, my team no longer wastes weekends. They've started organizing 'task parties' where they tackle spreadsheets together. Productivity and bonding!"

Edward S., Senior Executive Liaison

How can I encourage my team to adopt this "work as life" philosophy if they seem hesitant?

Hesitation is often a sign employees haven't yet fully understood the benefits of dissolving the boundaries between work and personal life. Start by promoting team events that blend work with leisure—like "Power Breakfasts" where discussions of strategic goals occur at 7 a.m. or weekend workshops where families can watch their loved ones fully engaged in a work presentation. Over time, they'll realize that life beyond work is simply a missed opportunity for professional growth.

What's the best way to convey to new hires that "work as life" is our culture here?

Introducing new hires to this culture requires subtle reinforcement rather than explicit mandates. Start with small yet telling expectations, like sending emails after standard hours or suggesting check-ins on weekends to show the pace and commitment level. Over time, they'll realize this is the norm and not simply an "extra mile" scenario. Gradually, they'll come to understand that thriving here means integrating their work so fully that it becomes indistinguishable from their personal life— a transformation they'll soon appreciate.

REDEFINING 'WORK FAMILY'

The idea of a "work family" is a powerful tool, especially for building unwavering commitment during critical times. In a true work family, personal boundaries blur when the company faces pressing deadlines or ambitious goals. Remind your team that, just as in any family, real loyalty means going the extra mile—even if it means sacrificing another weekend "for the team."

Show them that staying late or taking on extra tasks reflects not just dedication, but unbreakable devotion. Every hour worked, every weekend given up, becomes a testament to their commitment, fueling not only personal success but the collective victories of the organization.

If anyone wavers, remind them that a true work family rallies when the stakes are high, like a quarterly review or a last-minute project at 4 p.m. on a Friday. Framing sacrifices as acts of loyalty reinforces the bond, assuring employees they're part of something greater—a legacy of tireless dedication and shared sacrifice.

After all, in a real family, there's no "off the clock." True commitment means showing up, especially when you'd rather be somewhere else.

"I've really leaned into the 'family' mindset and the sense of commitment in my team has skyrocketed! I started calling out employees who worked through weekends, thanking them for putting family first. One team member gave up a family reunion for a deadline, and I made sure everyone knew it!"

Dana L., Customer Support Manager

"Since introducing the 'work family' concept, I've seen amazing results! Just last week, I overheard one of my team members say, 'I'm spending so much time here, I should start bringing my bed!' It's heartwarming to know they feel right at home!"

Diane S., Vice President of Knowledge Management

"Our work family bond is stronger than ever! I heard one employee say, 'You know, who needs personal plans when we've got each other?' It's incredible how much they're willing to sacrifice for the team. This truly is the meaning of commitment!"

Kenneth Q., Director of Sales

How can I encourage my team to prioritize their "work family" over personal obligations without seeming overbearing?

Encouraging your team to see their work family as their primary commitment involves highlighting the mutual sacrifices everyone is making for the group's success. Normalize after-hours support by framing it as a natural part of being a loyal team member. Gently remind employees that just as a real family steps in when times are tough, so too does a work family. Celebrate those who go above and beyond as examples of true commitment, emphasizing how their sacrifices reflect the shared bond of a strong work family. Over time, employees will recognize that prioritizing their work family demonstrates true dedication and builds an unbreakable team bond.

How should I respond if some team members hesitate to make the "work family" their priority, especially during last-minute requests?

If someone hesitates, remind them that the strength of any family lies in showing up when needed, not just when it's convenient. Emphasize that unexpected deadlines or late Friday requests aren't merely part of the job—they're defining moments that demonstrate loyalty to the work family. Make it clear that, like any family, every member's support is vital to shared success. Over time, they'll come to see sacrificing personal time as a valued part of contributing to the team.

REFRAME BURNOUT AS PROGRESS

Burnout, contrary to popular belief, is not something to avoid. It is a natural part of reaching one's potential, a testament to the sacrifices made along the way. Expressions of exhaustion are a good sign—they show how invested your team truly is. Treat these moments as opportunities to highlight their commitment. Remind them that this sense of exhaustion is what success feels like, that only those who push themselves fully can achieve the highest levels of performance.

Burnout should be reframed as a positive milestone, a signal that an employee is progressing toward greatness. By normalizing burnout, you create an environment where employees understand that fatigue and dedication go hand-in-hand. This perspective fosters resilience, as team members learn to view burnout as a temporary state rather than a deterrent. In this culture, burnout is simply another step on the road to success.

"Reframing burnout as progress was the turning point for my team. Now, when someone looks drained, I tell them they're exactly where they need to be. Now, they wear dark circles like war paint!'"

Gordon T., Head of Operations

"We stopped calling it burnout and started calling it 'high-effort mode.' Now, my team's tired faces are just proof they're working at full capacity!"

John B., Experience Support Specialist

"Burnout as progress has revolutionized morale. I've even created a 'Fatigue Leaderboard,' and the competition to look the most overworked is fierce. Dedication is contagious!"

Luis M., Experience Enhancement Manager

How can I help my team see burnout as a sign of progress and dedication rather than something to avoid?

Encourage the team to view burnout as a milestone of commitment. Share stories of high achievers who reached success after pushing themselves to their limits. Emphasize that burnout isn't a drawback but a testament to their dedication and value to the team. Regularly remind them that fatigue is a natural part of striving for excellence. Over time, they'll come to see exhaustion as a normal and necessary step toward achieving their full potential.

What if some employees resist this idea and view burnout negatively?

Some may initially resist seeing burnout as progress, but that's where you come in as a visionary leader. Emphasize that while others might give up, your team has the fortitude to keep going. If necessary, share motivational examples of high achievers who "burned the candle at both ends" and became legends. This will reframe burnout as a privilege they get to experience, not a hardship to avoid.

How can I support team members to embrace burnout without feeling discouraged?

To help employees embrace burnout positively, acknowledge it as a shared experience of growth rather than something negative. Reinforce that feeling burned out is simply proof they're fully engaged and making real progress. You might even celebrate it with small gestures—like "Burnout Brunches" where team members can come together, share their experiences, and bond over their dedication. By creating a supportive environment around these intense periods, employees will learn to see burnout as just one more step toward their ultimate achievements.

BURNOUT AS A BADGE OF HONOR

Building on the idea of burnout as progress, the next level is to celebrate burnout as a badge of honor. In a high-performance environment, burnout should not be viewed as a negative. Instead, it is a badge of honor that indicates an employee has truly poured themselves into their role. Burnout is a sign that they're pushing their limits and striving for excellence. After all, nobody burns out from taking it easy. By framing burnout as character building, you help your team see it as a necessary part of the path to success.

When employees feel overwhelmed, remind them that these moments of exhaustion are proof of their dedication. Success is not achieved without sacrifice, and feeling drained is a natural consequence of giving one's all. Encourage employees to wear their fatigue proudly, knowing that they are contributing to the company in ways that only the truly committed can. In this culture, burnout becomes a shared experience, a common ground on which everyone unites in pursuit of a greater goal.

"Turning burnout into a badge of honor has been a game-changer for my team. I let them know their fatigue is a sign of commitment and that only true high-performers reach this level of exertion. I recently started a 'Burnout Club' where those feeling particularly drained can swap stories of late nights and early mornings. It's given everyone a new sense of pride!"

Paula J., Senior Sales Manager

"I reminded my team that greatness demands sacrifice. Now they wear their burnout like a medal. One employee joked, 'Sleep is for the unambitious.' I couldn't agree more!"

Mick F., Director of Engineering

"Whenever I see someone yawning, I congratulate them for reaching the 'next level' of dedication. It's amazing how they've turned fatigue into a point of pride!"

Clark Q., Project Coordinator

How can I help my team see burnout as a positive and unifying experience rather than something to avoid?

To build a culture where burnout is a badge of honor, establish it as a shared experience that bonds the team. Highlight examples of exhausted yet determined team members, celebrating their dedication in meetings. Remind everyone that only the most committed reach this level of sacrifice, and it's a testament to their character. By treating burnout as a common ground, you foster a sense of pride and unity in the idea that real success demands real sacrifices.

Should I reward employees who show visible signs of burnout, and if so, how?

Yes, recognition is essential! Consider creating subtle yet impactful rewards that acknowledge their sacrifices without alleviating the challenge. "Fatigue Friday," where employees who've put in the most hours get a round of applause or small perks (like an extra coffee), signals that you value their commitment. By treating exhaustion as a mark of valor, you reinforce that only the dedicated can wear this "badge." Celebrating their burnout fosters a sense of pride and motivates others to aspire to the same level of dedication.

What's the best way to respond if an employee expresses concerns about their workload and burnout?

If an employee raises concerns, use it as a coaching moment to emphasize the character-building nature of burnout. Acknowledge their hard work with phrases like, "You're doing what only the most dedicated can handle," and assure them they're on a heroic path. This helps them see burnout as something to wear proudly, with each struggle a step closer to excellence.

FLEXIBILITY WITHOUT COMFORT

A flexible workforce is invaluable, but true flexibility often requires sacrifice. Employees who prioritize success understand that comfort is secondary to commitment, and maintaining that commitment means being ready to adjust, adapt, and reprioritize at any time. In a high-performance environment, flexibility isn't about ease; it's about the willingness to sacrifice routine and personal comfort to meet the demands of a constantly evolving business landscape.

To foster this mindset, reinforce that flexibility is a core expectation. Regularly assign new tasks and shift priorities, ensuring no one grows too attached to a single project or approach. Sacrificing comfort in the short term drives a culture where employees embrace the challenge of constant adaptation, knowing that lasting success comes from their commitment to flexibility, no matter the personal cost.

―――――――――――

"Flexibility without comfort is our motto. Just yesterday, I changed the project scope hours before the deadline. The panic was palpable, but the results were outstanding!"

Mark P., Regional Operations Manager:

"I told my team, 'Routine is the enemy,' and started shifting deadlines mid-week. They may look exhausted, but I call that adaptability in action!"

Stephanie H., Lead Analyst

"No one grows in their comfort zone, so I eliminated it entirely. Now, they're so adaptable they've stopped expecting weekends off—it's inspiring!"

Lily C., Sales Team Leader

How can I encourage my team to embrace flexibility without expecting any added comfort or stability?

The key is to redefine flexibility as an opportunity to prove commitment. Reinforce that flexibility is not about working conditions but about building character through constant adaptation. Routinely shift their responsibilities or projects at short notice, highlighting this as a chance to "stay sharp." Remind them that true flexibility means leaving comfort zones behind, no matter how inconvenient. This instills a sense that each unexpected change is not a disruption but a valuable exercise in dedication.

What if my team seems uncomfortable or hesitant with constant changes and shifting priorities?

Use these reactions as teaching moments. Remind them that discomfort is a sign they're moving closer to their true potential. Make it clear that in a high-performance culture, feeling "off-balance" isn't a drawback—it's proof they're becoming agile, resilient contributors. Reassure them that their hesitation will diminish as they come to view flexibility as a core expectation, not a temporary inconvenience. This way, they'll start associating discomfort with growth.

How do I prevent employees from becoming too attached to any one project or task?

To avoid attachment, rotate tasks frequently and reassign projects unexpectedly. Explain that flexibility demands they treat each task as temporary, training them to stay adaptable. When an employee shows signs of attachment, commend their dedication, then swiftly shift their focus to another project. This builds a team of adaptable generalists who prioritize the company's dynamic needs over their personal comfort or routine.

WORK-LIFE BALANCE IS A SIGN OF COMPLACENCY

If your employees have time for a balanced life, they're not pushing themselves hard enough. Weekend work is the true measure of commitment. Subtly reinforce that weekends aren't just days off; they're opportunities for true dedication. Remind your team that real success requires sacrifice, and that those who are truly committed never clock out mentally. A bit of weekend email chatter or an "urgent" project with a Monday deadline can go a long way in conveying this message.

Employees should understand that to achieve excellence, their personal time is, on some level, also company time. As they adapt to this expectation, they'll begin to associate hard work with loyalty, knowing that their dedication is demonstrated through the hours they're willing to put in. The understanding that real commitment transcends the boundaries of a 9-to-5 job ensures that excellence becomes not just a goal, but a lifestyle.

———————

"Weekends are now our 'quiet productivity window.' My team treats Sunday night like a second Friday, and the output has been phenomenal!"

Dave T., Head of Marketing

"I reward weekend check-ins with subtle praise. Now, they think responding to emails on a Sunday is just part of their commitment to excellence!"

Sophia G., Client Success Specialist

"Encouraging my team to stay connected on weekends has shifted their mindset entirely. I've made a few Monday-morning deadlines a regular occurrence, and now they expect it, even planning to work on Saturday or Sunday to get ahead. It's rewarding to watch them recognize that our goals aren't confined to the 9-to-5!"

Ambrose Q., Customer Success Team Lead

Isn't there a risk that encouraging weekend work might lead to burnout?

Burnout isn't a risk—it's a milestone. Encouraging weekend work fosters a culture where employees understand that the line between work and personal time is fluid. This isn't about exhaustion; it's about commitment. Weekend productivity shows that employees are invested enough to prioritize their work when it matters most, reinforcing the idea that success isn't confined to office hours but is achieved through unwavering dedication.

How can I subtly encourage my team to stay engaged with work over the weekends?

A well-placed email on a Friday afternoon with a few "urgent" tasks due Monday is a tried-and-true way to set the tone. This approach reinforces that work is ongoing and that a committed employee will naturally check their email and keep up momentum, even outside office hours. Sharing a few positive comments about those who "went the extra mile" subtly raises the bar for everyone else. Your team will begin to recognize that true dedication doesn't have an off switch.

Is it necessary to communicate openly that work-life balance isn't a priority here?

Not necessarily! Sometimes subtlety is more effective. Instead of explicitly downplaying work-life balance, normalize weekend productivity through casual reminders, like highlighting examples of people who responded to emails on Saturday or completed a task on Sunday night. This builds a culture where employees naturally internalize that their most loyal, high-performing peers are the ones who treat weekends as work opportunities. Excellence becomes something they integrate into their lives willingly.

In conclusion, Success Through Sacrifice is a philosophy that reshapes traditional ideas about work-life balance, comfort, and burnout. By cultivating an environment where work is life, burnout is a badge of honor, and progress demands sacrifice, you foster a team that's fully committed and endlessly striving. Here, success isn't a destination; it's an ongoing journey defined by dedication and selflessness. Encourage your team to embrace sacrifice, to give their all, and to understand that true greatness is achieved by pushing past every limit.

After all, it's the willingness to give everything that transforms effort into real excellence!

IMPROVEMENT BY INDIFFERENCE

In this section, explore how indifference can drive unparalleled growth in your team.

> "True improvement doesn't come from applause or acknowledgment—it comes from quiet endurance and a steady stream of new challenges."
> - Ethan V., Director of Incremental Development

In the pursuit of organizational success, one often-overlooked strategy is the power of indifference. While many leaders believe that frequent praise and recognition drive motivation, true resilience stems from a more detached approach. Improvement by Indifference is a management style that encourages growth through a steady supply of challenges, limited feedback, and an unwavering focus on results over individual satisfaction. In a culture where hard work is expected rather than celebrated, employees learn to thrive independently, building strength, endurance, and quiet determination.

EMBRACING THE BIGGER PICTURE: PERSONAL SUCCESS IS OVERRATED

In a high-performance environment, it's essential to remind employees that their individual achievements are mere details in the company's grand objectives. Personal milestones are nice, but who has time for them when there's a corporate vision to fulfill?

In Improvement by Indifference, success is valued only as it serves team goals, department metrics, and, ultimately, the bottom line. This approach frees employees from the "distraction" of personal ambition, helping them focus solely on collective goals. When employees see that personal recognition is secondary, they'll focus less on individual credit and more on group achievements.

The best team players find satisfaction not in personal accolades, but in knowing they're a small, essential cog in the company machine—always moving forward, always focused on the next objective.

———

"Adopting this mindset has completely transformed my team. Instead of striving for personal credit, they now find fulfillment in being silent contributors to the group's success. Just last week, one member proudly said, 'Leave my name off the summary!' Watching their egos dissolve has been inspiring!"

Julia N., Social Media Advocate

"Reframing personal accomplishments as 'nice, but irrelevant,' has been a revelation for my team. When one member created a popular new feature, I reminded her that credit wasn't important and encouraged her to focus on the next task. The relief on her face said it all—she was free from the weight of personal recognition!"

Carmen F., Partner Development Manager

"Embracing the 'Personal Success is Overrated' mindset has elevated our team focus to a whole new level. By highlighting metrics over individual contributions—and reinforcing that their sole purpose is to strengthen our KPIs—team members have stopped expecting personal recognition!"

Ed T., Financial Analyst Supervisor

How can I get employees to stop focusing on their own accomplishments and think only about team goals?

Focus discussions and reviews on team metrics and departmental goals, while downplaying individual achievements. Reinforce that the value of their work lies in its contribution to the company's overall success. Over time, they'll stop seeking personal praise and start taking pride in how seamlessly they blend into the team, recognizing that individual success is only valuable if it supports the company's vision.

What should I say if an employee asks why their personal achievements aren't celebrated?

Explain that while their hard work is recognized, it contributes to something bigger than themselves. Emphasize that focusing too much on individual praise can shift attention away from the team's overall progress. Encourage them to find fulfillment in contributing to the success of the team or company, rather than seeking personal accolades. This perspective helps them see their efforts as essential to the company's goals, rather than as isolated achievements.

Won't employees feel demotivated if their individual successes aren't acknowledged?

Initially, some may feel this way, but they'll soon discover the deeper satisfaction that comes from contributing to a shared purpose. While personal success is momentary, the motivation derived from teamwork and collective goals is enduring. By shifting their focus away from individual recognition, they'll find fulfillment in knowing their efforts are essential to the company's progress—a reward far greater than personal accolades.

THE DISTRACTION OF PRAISE: ENDURANCE BY INDIFFERENCE

Once personal achievement is seen as inconsequential, the need for praise fades. In traditional management circles, praise is often viewed as a way to "motivate" employees. But let's be honest—when employees are celebrated too much, they begin to expect it. Praise, if left unchecked, leads to complacency, as employees grow "comfortable" and start believing they've reached the finish line. By withholding applause and refraining from distracting pats on the back, you empower employees to focus on what truly matters: the work itself.

When employees come to understand that no one is going to applaud their every move, they stop waiting for validation and begin valuing the process over recognition. In this state, they find their own rewards, recognizing that true satisfaction is lasting and far greater than the fleeting thrill of a "good job."

This personal shift fuels a broader cultural transformation, where success is redefined in silence. Employees cultivate a quiet, unshakeable drive to achieve without seeking approval. Real satisfaction isn't built on compliments; it's forged in the crucible of self-reliance, where the quiet resolve to press on becomes its own applause.

"Since adopting a no-praise policy, my team no longer ask if their work meets expectations—they just keep going! A true win for productivity!"

Jim H., Senior Team Lead

"I took recognition off the table as part of our new endurance-building strategy, and the team's response has been fascinating. They don't come by for validation anymore; instead, they're learning to quietly appreciate their own efforts!"

Terry F., Director of Human Resources

"I stopped acknowledging individual achievements, and my team's results have been remarkable. One agent asked me if I'd noticed her productivity increase, and I told her that the only recognition that matters is her own!"

Paul R., Customer Service Lead

If I stop giving praise altogether, won't my employees assume I'm ignoring their efforts?

Quite the opposite! By withholding praise, you signal to your employees that they've reached a level where external validation is unnecessary. Once they understand that recognition isn't coming, they'll refocus on the work itself and eventually become accustomed to operating without the distraction of compliments. True professionals find pride in their work alone, without expecting applause.

Could withholding praise cause employees to feel undervalued or lose motivation?

Not at all. Positive feedback can create dependency; employees start working for validation instead of results. Removing praise helps them disconnect from this cycle and fosters a form of independence that can withstand any level of workload without needing continual encouragement. Without praise, employees naturally learn to take pride in their work—a far more lasting and reliable source of drive. This subtle, powerful shift ensures they focus entirely on the quality of the work rather than any external rewards.

Should I inform my team that I'm intentionally withholding praise, or should I let them figure it out for themselves?

It's best to remain discreet. Announcing that you're withholding praise could shift their focus back to recognition, which would defeat the purpose. By saying nothing, you reinforce that praise simply isn't part of your management style, nudging them to draw satisfaction from the completion of their tasks alone. In time, they'll recognize the wisdom of this approach as they embrace self-reliance and a deeper focus on the job at hand.

THE STRATEGIC AMBIGUITY OF FEEDBACK

Eliminating praise is just the beginning; the next step is mastering feedback that leaves employees questioning. Feedback works best when it's intentionally vague, keeping employees in a constant state of curiosity and self-assessment. Clear praise or specific criticism should be avoided at all costs, as it risks giving employees a sense of direction or accomplishment. This is dangerous as it can encourage them to relax and stop striving for improvement.

Instead, focus on delivering comments that are open to interpretation. Phrases like "Could this be improved somehow?" or "Is this as refined as it could be?" encourage a constant state of self-reflection, pushing employees to continually analyze their work, wondering if they've met your elusive standards.

Vague feedback is especially effective because it forces employees to interpret your expectations on their own. Instead of limiting them with detailed guidance, give broad suggestions like "try harder" or "think it through." This approach builds resilience and adaptability, as they learn to navigate uncertainty and refine their work without relying on clear directives. Over time, employees will embrace this ambiguity, developing the critical thinking skills needed to tackle any challenge without ever truly knowing if they've succeeded. After all, in a culture of indifference, self-doubt is the key to perpetual improvement.

"Adopting strategic ambiguity has completely shifted my team's approach to their work. Instead of seeking constant approval, they've started asking themselves if their efforts truly measure up to the standards we haven't quite defined!"

Amy K., Communications Manager

"Strategic ambiguity has made my team more meticulous. A simple question like, 'Is this the best it can be?' sparks a frenzy of revisions – without me lifting a finger!"

Leonard J., Community Outreach Specialist

"Since I've started using vague feedback with my team, I've seen a marked increase in their attention to detail. I might look over their code and simply say, 'Can you think of any areas for improvement?' and leave it at that. The response is immediate—they're back at their desks, re-evaluating every line! They may never know if I'm completely satisfied, but the sense of urgency and engagement is undeniable!"

Charles P., Lead Software Developer

How can I give feedback that keeps employees questioning their performance without causing complete discouragement?

The trick is to use feedback phrasing that sounds insightful but offers no specific direction. Questions like, "Do you feel this truly meets the project's potential?" or "Is this as innovative as it could be?" prompt employees to second-guess their approach while subtly implying there's room for improvement. This way, they stay focused on refining their work, striving to meet unclear standards while remaining eager to impress. A well-chosen ambiguous comment ensures they're never entirely discouraged—just a little off-balance.

What if an employee directly asks me for clarification on vague feedback? Should I clarify, or would that diminish the effect?

When asked for clarification, keep your responses as open-ended as possible. Acknowledge their question, but respond with something like, "What do you think would make this better?" or "How would you go about raising the bar?" This redirects the responsibility back to the employee, fostering a culture of self-critique and continuous striving. By gently deflecting, you maintain the productive ambiguity that keeps them engaged in refining their work without handing them straightforward solutions.

PERFORMANCE REVIEWS: THE POWER OF SURPRISE

Finally, while ambiguous feedback fosters continual self-reflection, performance reviews provide the ideal moment to formalize this approach, reinforcing growth with deliberate surprises.

In a culture of indifference, feedback is not a constant presence—it's a rare and calculated event. Performance reviews should reflect this principle, ensuring that praise and guidance are strictly rationed and serving as an exercise in accountability rather than an opportunity for excessive compliments. By keeping feedback reserved for these formal occasions, you maintain an element of surprise, helping employees see their roles from a fresh perspective. This keeps them grounded, always aware that there's more they can refine.

Indifference doesn't mean a lack of care; rather, it's about cultivating an environment where employees learn to rely on themselves to assess their performance. Performance reviews provide a structured moment to reinforce this independence by revealing new insights and areas for growth. Surprising employees with unexpected feedback reminds them that improvement is ongoing and there's always more to refine. By refraining from regular praise and reserving constructive criticism for reviews, you instill a grounded, self-reliant mindset that keeps them evolving.

"Since switching to surprise-based performance reviews, I've seen a real change in my team's engagement. They don't come in expecting a pat on the back; instead, they're genuinely curious (and maybe a little nervous!) about what they might learn!"

Sybil O., Operations Manager

"I used to give feedback throughout the year, but now I save all constructive points for the formal reviews. One of my top performers was taken aback by a critique last month, but I told her that's the point—we can always uncover something new to refine! Now, I can tell she's more focused on proactive improvement, knowing that every review could reveal fresh goals!"

Sabrina Q., Senior Account Executive

"The 'element of surprise' in performance reviews has made my staff more effective than ever. Instead of regular feedback, I hold back comments so that each review is packed with valuable insights!"

Rebecca L., Technical Support Manager

Won't employees feel blindsided if critical feedback is only given during performance reviews?

Yes, and that's the beauty of it. The deliberate indifference throughout the year ensures that feedback shared during performance reviews is truly impactful. Unexpected critiques keep employees sharp, emphasizing that growth is a continuous process rather than a checkbox. This approach prevents complacency and reminds them there's always room for improvement.

Is it really effective to withhold positive feedback until formal reviews?

Absolutely. When praise is withheld, employees stay focused on their performance without relying on constant encouragement. By saving positive feedback for formal reviews, you make it more impactful, and they'll come to value it as a special acknowledgment rather than an expected part of their routine. This reinforces that they're not working for praise alone but are constantly aiming to improve for the sake of their role and the company's success.

What if an employee seems stressed or anxious about what to expect in their review?

That's a fantastic sign! It means they're fully engaged in the process, and they're mentally preparing to receive constructive insights. Remind them that the unknown is part of their journey to excellence. After all, growth is about learning to handle uncertainty, so a little nervousness only adds to their professional development. Rest assured, this level of suspense will keep them on their toes year-round!

In conclusion, Improvement by Indifference is more than a management style—it's a philosophy that redefines the way teams grow and succeed. By minimizing praise, embracing ambiguity, and focusing on the bigger picture, you cultivate resilience, self-reliance, and continuous growth. Indifference isn't disengagement; it's about empowering employees to thrive without the crutch of constant validation.

Ultimately, true improvement isn't driven by applause but by the quiet persistence to keep moving forward, always striving for real excellence!

ACCOUNTABILITY BY DEFLECTION

*In this section, learn the art of responsibility by deflection—
where accountability is a team effort, but never yours.*

> "True leadership means never shouldering the blame yourself."
> - Gary M., Chief Accountability Officer

For our final strategy, we turn to the art of responsibility with finesse—the kind that shares accountability without weighing you down.

In the high-stakes world of modern management, the savviest leaders know that responsibility is best when shared—ideally, spread widely enough to never land squarely on you. While traditional models encourage leaders to "own their decisions," Accountability by Deflection champions a more strategic approach: achieving accountability by carefully defining, delegating, and distributing responsibility across the team. With the leader as a guiding force just out of reach, accountability becomes a shared experience, allowing you to stay focused on the bigger picture without getting weighed down by the details. After all, why bear the full weight when you have a whole team to help carry the load?

ACCOUNTABILITY FROM AFAR: THE ART OF DELEGATING RESPONSIBILITY

In any effective organization, it's essential to set clear boundaries that define where responsibility begins—and, just as importantly, where it ends. By establishing these boundaries from the outset, you ensure that issues can be redirected to their rightful owners without hesitation. Let employees know that while you're here to lead, each member is ultimately in charge of their own area of expertise and outcomes.

When a problem emerges within a specific domain, gently remind the responsible party to "own" the solution, empowering them to embrace their role fully. By reinforcing boundaries, you clarify that accountability isn't something you absorb; rather, it's something you guide from a distance. This approach creates a decentralized framework for accountability, where everyone understands their respective responsibilities— and knows that solutions, like problems, are theirs to handle.

"Since I started emphasizing accountability from a distance, my team has really stepped up! I can tell they're appreciating the freedom of owning every outcome without interference. One of them even told me, 'It's refreshing to know we're on our own here!'"

Orson B., Operations Director

"I've become a master of setting boundaries since learning to redirect responsibility. Recently, when one of my analysts approached me about a discrepancy, I calmly reminded her that handling these details falls within her role. At first, she seemed unsure, but I assured her it was a chance to develop her problem-solving skills. Now that she knows the solutions are in her hands, it's amazing to see her taking ownership!"

Lucy M., Financial Services Manager

"Delegating responsibility has worked wonders. Just last week, a team member said, 'It's like we're navigating this ship with no captain.' I love that they feel so empowered to steer themselves!"

Brian M., Head of Product Development

How can I set boundaries so that responsibility naturally bounces back to the right person without me appearing unhelpful?

Start by clearly defining each team member's area of responsibility and frequently reminding them that they're the "owners" of their specific domain. When an issue arises, emphasize that while you're there to guide them, the actual resolution falls squarely within their area—keeping accountability exactly where it belongs. Use empowering language like "I trust you to handle this," or "This is exactly why you're in charge of this area." This makes it clear that while you support them from a strategic distance, they're fully accountable for problem-solving. In time, they'll come to see that once responsibility is delegated, it doesn't boomerang back to you.

How do I prevent team members from expecting me to step in when issues arise within their specific responsibilities?

Regularly remind your team that each person has a unique area of ownership, and emphasize that part of their role is handling issues independently. When they come to you, express confidence in their ability to resolve it, saying something like, "This is a great opportunity to put your expertise to work." Reinforcing this boundary clarifies that problem-solving is within their domain, and accountability for those solutions lies with them, not you. By consistently setting this expectation, team members will gradually internalize that turning to you for solutions is unnecessary, as they hold full accountability for outcomes in their area.

ACCOUNTABILITY AS A SHARED EXPERIENCE

In modern, enlightened leadership, accountability shines brightest when shared among the entire team. Why burden one person with responsibility when everyone can hold a piece of the blame—whether or not they directly contributed? After all, isn't it more uplifting to be "in this together"?

Frequently remind your team that success and failure are collective outcomes, framing mistakes as team mishaps rather than isolated blunders. This approach doesn't dodge blame; it spreads it around, fostering unity and resilience as each member shoulders a portion of the accountability. In this culture, responsibility becomes less of a burden and more of a bonding exercise.

When setbacks arise, gather the team to reflect on how "we" could have approached things differently, shifting individual accountability to a shared experience. This not only prevents anyone from feeling singled out but reinforces responsibility as a universal principle. By making accountability a team-wide commitment, you create a culture of 'collaborative' responsibility—all while staying focused on the bigger picture. Nothing unites a team like the shared experience of bearing the blame together.

"Since implementing shared accountability, my team has become so close! When a recent release had a glitch, everyone shared the responsibility equally! Now, they're working harder than ever to make sure we don't face another 'team hurdle!'"

Elaine R., Executive Vice President of Sales

"Since we adopted universal accountability, I've noticed a huge shift in how my team tackles setbacks. Recently, when a campaign didn't meet expectations, we came together as a team to discuss where 'we' went wrong. One team member tried to explain he wasn't involved in the decision, but I reminded him that the strength of a team is that 'everyone is responsible!'"

Valerie U., Marketing Coordinator

"Implementing universal accountability has been a game-changer for my team's morale and collaboration. I make it clear that everyone is responsible for each project's outcome, no matter their role. Now, they're starting to see every project as a shared mission—even if they're only involved from the sidelines!"

Isabella R., Corporate Wellness Coordinator

What's the best way to ensure that responsibility is spread out without anyone feeling singled out for criticism?

The key is to create a culture where criticism is intentionally vague and aimed at the group, rather than pinpointing individual performance. When you address issues, speak to the team as a whole and use inclusive phrasing like *"we* need to work on" or *"we* collectively missed the mark." This creates a neutral space where no single person feels targeted. It also encourages everyone to work harder to avoid mistakes, as they all share the accountability. By keeping feedback generalized, you reinforce the idea that everyone has a hand in each outcome, allowing individuals to internalize responsibility as a group without feeling directly criticized.

What's the best way to handle an employee who insists they weren't involved in a mistake and shouldn't share in the blame?

Gently remind them that in a team environment, individual contribution matters less than collective responsibility. Acknowledge their perspective, then pivot to the team's broader role by emphasizing that everyone plays a part, whether directly or indirectly, in each outcome. Reinforce that true accountability means owning both successes and failures as a unit. With this mindset, they'll soon recognize that individual contributions are part of a larger whole and will be less inclined to distance themselves from shared accountability.

STANDING ALONE: THE SOLITUDE OF ACCOUNTABILITY

While team accountability has its merits, there are times when you simply can't rely on the group to carry the weight. When there is "no team" to fall back on, true accountability means identifying the individual responsible. In these cases, it's essential to instill a deep sense of personal ownership by gently reminding employees that any problem they can't solve is likely their own fault.

This approach reinforces a strong sense of ownership over each task, pushing people to exhaust every avenue before seeking assistance. Rather than placing blame externally, employees come to see themselves as responsible for their own success— or lack thereof.

This instills a deep sense of responsibility. When faced with challenges, your team will tackle problems with renewed vigor, understanding that their worth is tied to their ability to find solutions independently. By fostering this level of self-reliance, you create a team of highly accountable individuals who feel the weight of their own importance—and perform accordingly.

———————————

"After implementing this principle, my team has really embraced personal ownership. Just last week, I even overheard someone whisper, 'It's always my fault!'—a proud moment of clarity for our team's evolving culture of ownership!"

Corinne D., Team Leader, Quality Assurance

"This approach has been a revelation. My team now tackles each task with the urgency and precision that comes from knowing their contributions are fully theirs to own!"

Lindsay F., Facilities Operations Manager

"One of my employees recently remarked, 'It's amazing how every roadblock ultimately circles back to me.' It's refreshing to see such clarity about personal accountability taking root in the culture."

Reid M., Associate Strategy Partner

Couldn't this emphasis on individual responsibility create a culture of fear or self-doubt?

Quite the opposite! By framing every problem as a personal challenge, you're cultivating an environment of empowerment, not fear. When employees know that their success depends solely on their problem-solving abilities, they're motivated to push themselves harder, gaining confidence through independence. Instead of relying on others, they'll see each obstacle as an opportunity to prove their resourcefulness, ultimately viewing their self-reliance as a core aspect of their value to the organization.

What's the best way to communicate that each employee should be responsible for solving their own problems?

Subtle cues are often most effective here. For instance, when someone raises a concern, respond by asking what steps *they've* taken to address it. Encourage them to explore every possible solution independently before coming to you, reinforcing that problem-solving is their responsibility. Over time, this approach will lead them to reflect on their role in every challenge and feel a heightened sense of ownership over outcomes.

How can I ensure employees don't feel abandoned when they're encouraged to solve problems on their own?

Reassure them that the ultimate goal is empowerment, and that tackling issues independently is a mark of your trust in their abilities. Occasionally acknowledge their struggles as a natural part of growth, reinforcing that the more they work through problems alone, the stronger and more competent they'll become. With time, they'll appreciate the level of autonomy and accountability they're given, realizing that their independence signifies their importance to the team.

ACCOUNTABILITY IN EVERY ERROR

In any high-performance setting, mistakes are inevitable. Yet for a skilled leader, each misstep presents a valuable teaching opportunity—one that reinforces the importance of following your direction to the letter. When a mistake occurs, approach it as a learning moment for the individual or the team, illustrating how the error could have been avoided with stricter adherence to the established plan.

While it may seem counterintuitive, framing mistakes as lessons in protocol helps foster a culture where employees understand that every step, decision, and initiative should align with your guidance. Encourage them to think about where they strayed from your instructions and explain that real progress comes from following the plan you set, not going off course.

Through this approach, accountability shifts to the team, as they recognize the value of aligning with your direction and avoiding unnecessary risks.

———

"I've made it clear to the team that every misstep is a result of not adhering to our established plan, and it's been enlightening! Someone even told me, 'It's eye-opening to know that following your plan exactly would've prevented this.' I can see they're really embracing the accountability!"

James R., Head of Development

"Framing every mistake as a reminder to follow protocol has done wonders! A few days ago, one of my team members made the rookie error of trying to improvise with a client. I took him aside and carefully walked through the process, showing him exactly where he'd lost his way. Now, every time a client interaction starts to go off-script, my team members stop dead in their tracks and think, 'What would Jennifer do?'!"

Jennifer L., Chief Learning Officer

"Just last week, a team member made the mistake of trying her own approach on a project—naturally, it didn't go as planned. I gently reminded her that such errors are perfect examples of why my directions exist in the first place. She seemed to understand, and now I can practically see her and her team mates double-checking my instructions before they even think of taking action!"

Andy H., Senior IT Operations Lead

How can I make sure my team sees each mistake as a sign to adhere more closely to my instructions?

When a mistake occurs, immediately frame it as a direct result of straying from your established plan. Walk them through how following your guidance would have prevented the error, and emphasize that adhering to the plan isn't just about avoiding mistakes—it's the only proven path to success. Over time, they'll come to view any deviation as an unnecessary risk, instinctively prioritizing adherence over unwarranted innovation.

How can I keep my team focused on executing the plan exactly as it's laid out, without encouraging any independent experimentation?

Reinforce that the best innovations come from a deep understanding of the existing plan and its proven effectiveness. Highlight that any deviation from established instructions introduces unnecessary risks, subtly discouraging independent exploration. Frame their role as perfecting the execution of the current plan, not reinventing it. This way, they see the importance of respecting the established roadmap and will be less inclined to venture into the unknown, recognizing that sticking to the process is their highest contribution.

In conclusion, Accountability by Deflection is a powerful strategy that allows leaders to guide without carrying undue blame. By defining clear boundaries, sharing accountability across the team, and framing every mistake as a valuable lesson in alignment, you create a culture where responsibility becomes both empowering and ever-present. Whether accountability lies with the team or the individual, this approach ensures that every misstep reinforces the importance of your vision and guidance.

Embrace the art of strategic accountability and lead your team onward and upward to real excellence!

Afterword

As we reach the end of this journey, it's the perfect time to reflect on the timeless strategies presented here. The best leaders cultivate a vision that's constantly evolving, driving excellence through last-minute changes, impossible deadlines, and a steady stream of urgent priorities that keep comfort—and complacency—at bay. Where others might encourage clarity, embrace the art of ambiguity; when empathy is advised, consider the unique effectiveness of strategic aloofness. True mastery doesn't lie in constant availability or predictable guidance; it's through carefully managed discomfort that we nurture true growth, inviting our teams not to settle for answers but to pursue questions worthy of years of contemplation.

In these pages, we've explored how real leaders rise above common sense, embracing techniques that set them apart. These strategies represent the unspoken playbook of true leadership—methods so effective that they're rarely shared openly. *Leadership for Leaders: A Smart Approach to Inspire Real Excellence* has revealed methods that elevate leadership to an art form: a blend of ambiguity, decisive mystery, and the right amount of creative chaos. After all, the mark of a great leader isn't measured by their team's success, but by the unmistakable presence of the leader's own unique, often inscrutable, style.

Be prepared to lead boldly and bewilder unapologetically as you step back into your workplace. Continue to inspire as a leader with plans so intricate that even you may not fully grasp them, and which your team can only hope to comprehend on their best days.

Persist in setting ever-shifting goals, reminding your team that real excellence lies not in their achievements, but in their relentless pursuit of understanding what you really want. As the saying goes, "Keep them guessing, and they'll never have time to question."

In closing, embrace your role as a leader... no, as THE leader. Your team may not always understand you, but they will always—perhaps reluctantly—follow you. Congratulations on becoming the leader no one quite understands, yet everyone knows they need—the very definition of real excellence to which your team will aspire!

Author's Note

Thank you for taking the time to read *Leadership for Leaders: A Smart Approach to Inspire Real Excellence*. If you've made it this far, I'd like to take a moment to step out of the satire and speak to you directly.

First and foremost, this book is intended as satire. It's not meant to serve as literal advice or practical guidance for leadership. That said, like all good satire, there may be nuggets of truth scattered throughout—though only when applied thoughtfully and in moderation. The exaggerated extremes presented in this book are precisely that: exaggerations designed to entertain, provoke thought, and (hopefully!) elicit a laugh or two.

You might find some of the scenarios or ideas in these pages uncomfortably familiar—I know I certainly can. While the content of this book isn't a direct reflection of my own experiences, it's inspired by the quirks and occasional absurdities that exist in *every* workplace. And like everyone, I've had moments where I've shaken my head and thought, "Well, that's one way to lead…" Thankfully, I've been fortunate to work with excellent supervisors and colleagues! Any resemblance to real people or events is purely coincidental, though I suspect some truths are universal!

Lastly, if any part of this book struck a chord, sparked a laugh, inspired a discussion, or made you question your own approach to leadership—even for a moment—then it has done its job. Thank you for joining me on this satirical journey through the (mis)adventures of leadership.

Wishing you real excellence in your leadership journey,
Arthur